Schooling Bodies

Schooling Bodies

School Practice and Public Discourse, 1880–1950

David Kirk

Leicester University Press
London and Washington

Leicester University Press

A Cassell Imprint
Wellington House, 125 Strand, London WC2R 0BB

PO Box 605, Herndon, Virginia, 20172-0605

First published 1998

© David Kirk 1998

British Library Cataloguing in Publication Data
A catalogue record for this book is available from the British Library.

ISBN   0–7185–0100–4

Library of Congress Cataloging-in-Publication Data
Kirk, David, 1958–
Schooling bodies : school practice and public discourse, 1880–1950 / David Kirk.
p.   cm.
Includes bibliographical references and index.
ISBN   0-7185-0100-4
1. Physical education and training—Australia—History—19th century.
2. Physical education and training—Australia—History—20th century.
3. Physical education and training—Great Britain—History—19th century
4. Physical education and training—Great Britain—History—20th century. I. Title.
GV315.K57 1998
613.7'071'041—dc21   97–33451
                                                                 CIP

Designed and typeset by Ben Cracknell Studios

Printed and bound in Great Britain by Bookcraft (Bath) Ltd,
Midsomer Norton, Somerset

Contents

For Annie, Calum and Murray

Introduction

What are now known, variously, as departments of human movement studies, sport science and kinesiology in universities and other institutions of higher education in Australia and Britain have a collective modern history that stretches back to the 1890s. These organizations along with the work of many private individuals and groups have been a repository of knowledge of the body that has been all but ignored by researchers of the body in society. This knowledge of the body might be amenable to analysis and explanation within the nowadays familiar theoretical frameworks belonging to fields such as anatomy, physiology, biomechanics and motor control, sociology, anthropology, philosophy and history, but it is not merely reducible to these frameworks. My own feeling is that scholars have overlooked this store of knowledge of the moving body as much due to this amenability to disciplinary analyses, and especially to the tendency for biophysical scientific frameworks to be foregrounded in such analyses, as to any intellectual snobbery deriving from the dominance of Cartesian dualism on western systems of thought – though I have no doubt that the snobbery remains alive and well.

If we must give a name to this stock of knowledge, we might reasonably call it physical training or perhaps physical education. Certainly, educational institutions such as schools have been primary sites in which this knowledge has been produced and reproduced, and until the 1970s education remained the major application of this knowledge, even in settings other than schools. A core concern of physical education, as this book attempts to recount, has been to produce particular, socially sanctioned movements in young people that relate to the physical competencies required of them as compliant citizens and productive workers. Given that these broad categories are differently defined according to the prevailing gender order, physical education has been a key site for the production of gendered bodies.

Now it might be argued that children learn to move competently and efficiently without access to physical education, and indeed this is so. Nevertheless, this fact has not deterred colonial and then state and federal governments in Australia and many other governments of western nations from utilizing physical activities in educational settings as a primary means of schooling bodies. This book is an attempt to explain why this has been so, why it is that bodies have been both a medium for schooling and a project of schooling. Along the way, I hope to show that schooling bodies has been integral to their social construction, which I take to denote a generic category that is not concerned with the biology of the body but rather with its simultaneous enmeshment in culture.

I will also try to show, for those interested in the body in society, that physical education might properly be described as a field of corporeal knowledge that provides valuable insights into the social construction of bodies. The field of physical education as I shall describe it, manifest in this book in the form of physical training, sport and games, and in the allied field of medical inspection, deals with somatic knowledge, with the kinesthetics of movement, of how the body's capabilities might be calculated and what these may be worth, of how it feels to move in particular ways and how these movements can be known and learned. The range of this knowledge is impressive, representing a panorama that stretches from the various early systems of 'rational gymnastics', that scrutinized and reconstructed in a pedagogical form just about every gross and many fine muscular movements of the body, through to competitive team games, that involved physically dynamic, rule-bound and complex forms of social play-like interactions.

The book can be read at a number of levels. It is, for all intents and purposes, a 'history' of physical training, medical inspection and sport in schools between the 1880s and the 1940s in Australia, with specific reference to parallel British developments. The historical record of schooling bodies during this period almost completely omits reference to Aboriginal bodies, and where they are not ignored, Aboriginal people are most often maligned or marginalized in this record. Since many of the school practices described in this text were saturated with concerns for race, this is a significant omission. Indigenous Australians thus can be part of this story only in terms of their absence. I can therefore make no claims to comprehensiveness for this history, and acknowledge with no little regret that it is an Anglo-Celtic history of physical education in Australia. I also acknowledge that there are some more detailed accounts of physical education in masters and doctoral theses languishing in various Australian university libraries. In cognizance of the fact there are no readily accessible, published book-length accounts of the history of physical education and school sport in Australia, I have tried to deal with the major events in this history. Having said this, the narrative is also intended to serve as a vehicle for the theoretical arguments of the book.

At one level the book explores the interrelationships between school practices, specifically those practices that school bodies explicitly, and the public discourses that collectively attempt to make sense of life at any given period in time, out of which these school practices are constructed and to

2

which they in turn contribute. At another level, an argument of the book is that the shifts in school practices during this period, particularly those associated with physical training, medical inspection and sport and games, provide some insights into broader shifts in what Foucault called biopower. I will try to convince the reader that the emergence and consolidation of militarized physical training and school medical inspection by the end of the first decade of this century represented both the ultimate achievement and the beginning of the decline of a phase of modernity Foucault describes as disciplinary society. New processes of schooling bodies began to emerge in the 1920s and 1930s, but these only started to make an impact on school practices in the 1940s. I suggest that these new practices that had games and sport in the vanguard signalled the coming of a new form of biopower that was, compared with the practices of disciplinary society instantiated in meticulous, precise and ponderous forms of schooling bodies, increasingly individualized, internalized and diffused.

As with most historical texts, the narrative is organized in this one in a roughly chronological sequence that deals first with the pre-First World War period, then with the interwar period, and finally with the period immediately proceeding the Second World War. However, individual chapters do not deal with these periods in time discretely, taking up where the previous one left off. Rather, each chapter overlaps and follows through issues across these periods in time. This organization of the text is intended to signal that behind the narrative, the treatment of progress and of change takes the form it does in order to assist coherence, while in fact there is no immutable progress of events, nor is there ever an even process of change. It should however be clear from this narrative that change is invariably the product of contestation and struggle over material and discursive resources that are most often unjustly and unevenly distributed and unequally accessed.

I make no claims to comprehensiveness in this history of the part played by physical training, medical inspection and sport and games in schooling bodies; I have drawn on material that was most accessible to me during the last six years. Much of this is from the state of Victoria, although I have made every effort to provide comparisons with other Australian states where I have felt this is warranted. Because of my interest in British developments and their special relationship to events in Australia, I have made selective comparisons, again where I have felt these might provide some points of orientation for the reader. I have also made clear reference to those histories that do provide more comprehensive or detailed coverage of specific events than I have been able to here, with the hope that the reader may find in these corroboration of the arguments I have presented in this book.

I wish to express my gratitude to Barbara Spiller and Karen Twigg who worked with me as research assistants on the projects on which this book is based. The book is the result of a reworking of some previously published material and its integration with new material. I wish to acknowledge with gratitude and thanks the permission given by editors of the following journals for the reproduction of some text from these articles: *Discourse, The Australian Journal of Education, History of Education Review, History of Education, Journal of Australian Studies,* and *Sporting Traditions.* Much of the initial research for this book was carried out at Deakin University, and I acknowledge their support, particularly in the form of research grants in 1991 and 1992. My current employer, The University of Queensland, has also made a significant contribution to the production of this book by granting me a teaching-free semester in 1997, and I thank my colleagues in the Department of Human Movement Studies for their generous support during this period. Finally, I wish to acknowledge the continuing support of my family, Sue, Murray, Annie and Calum, and their patience, encouragement and understanding, without which this book would never have seen the light of day.

David Kirk
Brisbane, May 1997

1

Schooling Bodies

> In arranging a scheme of drill at assembly, care must be taken that no class shall interfere with the drill of the other classes in the front, rear or flank; therefore, the school will probably have to be arranged in two columns. The classes in each column must be placed at least at column distance (the depth of the class), and the movements, confined almost to this limited area, should be so arranged that, at the close, the class will be on the line of the original formation. For concerted movements, classes will require to move to the same flank; whether left or right will depend on the arrangement of the drill ground . . . The infants should be drilled separately, and, for the junior classes, easier movements should be substituted for the diagonal march, squad marching in file, and forming up into squad. The scheme embraces the drill appointed for State Schools up to company drill.[1]

Writing in the *Education Gazette* of 1903, head teacher Mr Carter described for his readers the way in which morning assembly was organized at Maryborough State School, a government elementary school located in the north-west of the newly founded Australian state of Victoria. He commented that once the school had been arranged in space, each class and each child in their rightful place, the timing of events could be detailed. At 9 a.m. the first bell announced the commencement of the school day, followed by a second bell at 9.15 that signalled the beginning of assembly, which should cease ringing at precisely 9.16, at which point, as children turned towards the flag-pole and stood to attention, a first whistle was blown signalling the beginning of drill, then a second, third, fourth and fifth, each requiring specific actions on the part of children and teachers. Mr Carter carefully set out the exact movements to be accomplished by the classes, and the order in which these should be performed. A sixth whistle, blown at precisely 9.20, indicated that assembly was over and the children should return to the classroom. Once inside

> Children march to their places, halt, and remain standing in file.
> Right (left) turn.
> Cover files.

First Signal – 'Step.'
Second Signal – 'In.'
Caution – 'Hats.'
First Signal – Right incline.
    (Hats are passed by numbers.)
Second Signal – First desk to second desk.
Third Signal – Second desk to third desk.
Fourth Signal – Third desk to fourth desk.
Fifth Signal – Hats hung up.
Sixth Signal – Left incline.
Double Signal – Hands folded behind.
The teacher commences the first lesson.[2]

And so a day in the life of Maryborough State School would begin.

While a contemporary school administrator might consider Mr Carter's approach to the conduct of school assembly to be a little over-zealous, he was very much in tune with his time. Clearly impressed by prevailing military practices of marching and squad drilling, his detailed attention to the arrangement of children's bodies in space shows that Mr Carter had grasped the relationship between the ordering of space and the regulation of behaviour whereby he could, in Foucault's words, minimize the possibility of 'unusable and dangerous coagulations'.[3] Moreover, his precise time-tabling of the events that made the school day routinized and predictable ensured children were always purposefully occupied and reveals a time-consciousness embedded in the practices of capitalist production.[4]

Mr Carter's meticulous, detailed and precise concern for the uses of space and time was not confined to the assembly, but was instead a pervasive characteristic of both private schooling and compulsory mass schooling in the late nineteenth and early twentieth centuries. In all facets of school life, in the classroom and the playground, in the gymnasium and on the playing field, and in the corridors, stairways and pathways that joined these places, space and time were organized to regulate behaviour. This concern for the precise and detailed ordering of human activity in space and time was so pervasive that it might reasonably be described as a defining feature of schooling as it emerged as an institutionalized social practice in Australia, Britain and elsewhere.

We might also note that this precise ordering of space and time involved working on embodied children. It was children 'in the round' who were required to stand in file, to salute the flag, to hang their hats by numbers, to sit, stand and march in a certain way, to write and speak and read in a particular style, and who were sometimes physically punished for trans-gressions of these required ways of conducting themselves. Children's bodies were the subject matter of this precise attention to the ordering of space and time because it was here, to paraphrase Philip Corrigan,[5] that 'terror, fear and bodily turmoil' resided, in children's embodied experiences of schooling.

Corrigan claims that 'bodies matter schooling'. The language of 'terror, fear and bodily turmoil' is in part a response to the pushing, cuffing, punching and kicking, name-calling and ridiculing that formed an inevitable part of many children's experiences of schooling. But this is not all that Corrigan meant by his claim that bodies matter schooling. It is also the case that the regulative practices constituting schooling require ways of conducting oneself that are experienced in powerfully and profoundly physical ways by children. More than this, since all bodies bear the biological characteristics of femaleness and maleness, schooling bodies is enmeshed in the gender order and schooling actively differentiates embodied femininities and masculinities.

This proposal that bodies matter schooling may be viewed as controversial in the face of volumes of educational theory that 'never mentions bodies'.[6] Yet, despite the absence of the body in so much writing about education and schooling, it is clear Mr Carter and his peers had few doubts that work on the embodied child, and the regulation of children's bodies in space and in time, was central to the work of schools.

Almost forty years before Mr Carter's advice to his fellow teachers was published, Gustav Techow wrote in his 1866 volume *Manual of Gymnastic Exercises for the Use of Schools and at Home* that only a 'systematic culture of the muscles' could 'counter-balance the pernicious influences of civilised life'.[7] Techow was a leading physical culturist of the day, of Prussian extraction and resident in the colony of Victoria. What he meant by the phrase 'a systematic culture of the muscles' is outlined in intricate detail in terms of the spacing, alignment and subdivision of groups of bodies from each other, with minute descriptions of the exercises to be performed.

Perhaps one example from Techow's manual, a description of the 'fundamental position' of the gymnast from which all exercises start and finish, may suffice to show why school administrators such as Mr Carter, some forty years later, could seem convinced that corporeal regulation was part of the core business of schooling. According to Techow, the fundamental position of the gymnast required 'the shoulders and body' to be 'square to the front'

the heels in line and closed, the knees straight and firmly braced back; the feet turned out so as to form an angle of sixty degrees, the arms straight down from the shoulders, the elbows turned in and close to the sides so as to bring the palms of the hands full to the front, the five fingers close together, the hips and shoulders drawn back, the chest advanced, the body straight and inclining forward so as to have its weight bearing on the fore part of the feet, the head erect without being thrown back, the eyes straight to the front.[8]

It is worth taking a few moments to try to follow these instructions and to adopt Techow's fundamental position of the gymnast, just to feel what it is like to stand in this way, and then to begin to imagine this as the root position of a whole range of flexion and extension exercises of the head and neck, trunk, arms and legs. As in all other aspects of his work as a gymnast, Techow was quite precise in what he meant by the phrase 'a systematic culture of the muscles'; he meant that the development of corporeal regulation through a system of physical culture was a central, essential, indeed, constitutive, element of a well-ordered society.

While Techow, as we shall see, was to have mixed fortunes in persuading the colonial government of Victoria to adopt his system of gymnastics in state schools, his system and his views on its relationship to the constitution of society reflected widespread currents of thought developing in Europe and Britain. Other systems of 'rational gymnastics' such as those emerging during the nineteenth century from the work of Maclaren in England, Ling in Sweden and Jahn in Germany, had in common a concern for ordering the embodied subject in space and in time, whether adult or child, and shared the view that corporeal regulation through such activity formed the bedrock of a well-ordered and productive society.[9] Despite Techow's limited ability to influence some specific educational policy directions of the day, it seems clear that school administrators such as Mr Carter were drawing on well-established and widely held views on corporeal regulation that supported a concept of education that was centrally concerned with schooling bodies.

But how could these physical culturists and school administrators believe that their work had some relevance to social practices beyond their immediate spheres of influence? Why was it, for instance, that during their morning assembly the children of Maryborough State School stood to attention and faced the Australian flag while it was raised? Why was Mr Carter so keen to timetable the order of events during assembly so precisely? And why did he consider military drill to be an appropriate ingredient of an elementary school assembly? How could Gustav Techow, in his 1866 text, feel justified in making the claim that a systematic culture of the muscles could right the wrongs of society and that 'symmetry and equilibrium of the body and mind . . . are the secret foundation of individual success and of national greatness'?[10]

We can catch a glimpse both in Mr Carter's advice and in Techow's writing of a range of public discourses, of militarism, nationalism, and capitalism, that have no specific relationship to schooling but nevertheless provide some of the discursive resources that construct and constitute school practices. Moreover, we can glimpse in Mr Carter's description of school assembly evidence of the instantiation of these discursive practices. If bodies mattered schooling during the last decades of the nineteenth century and early decades of this century, what relationship did schools have to the social order and the myriad discursive practices that constructed and constituted it? The answers to these questions lie in part in comprehending the nature of public discourse prevailing at the time, which we will come to shortly, and in part in grasping the concept of the socially constructed body.

The Social Construction of Bodies

The social construction of bodies has in the last ten years emerged as a topic of increasing significance in social research. This scholarly interest in the body has covered a wide and diverse range of topics and has now generated a sufficiently large literature to warrant the publication of review articles and introductory textbooks.[11] While we might argue about the most adequate ways in which to discuss bringing society into the body and the body into society, there appears to be an increasingly widespread understanding of the notion that the body is as much a social as it is a biological phenomenon, existing simultaneously in culture and nature.

This new work on the body in society has already demonstrated a potential to liberate our thinking from the tyranny of Cartesian dualism[12] and in so doing to offer persuasive arguments that the body is integral to understanding the development and constitution of society.[13] At the same time, a problem with much of this work is that it has tended in the main to lack a historical perspective.[14] One of the consequences of this becomes all too apparent when we consider David Lowenthal's claim in *The Past is a Foreign Country* that 'nostalgia is today the universal catchword for looking back'.[15] According to Lowenthal, lack of detailed attention to historical evidence allows pasts to be manufactured so that they can be enjoyed nostalgically. Not only does this process construct pasts that are often used to legitimate oppressive practices in the present,[16] it also obscures the relationships between past, present and future by asserting that the past is a foreign place that can only be comprehended dimly, a place somehow richer yet simpler and better than the present.

Social critic Philip Adams has claimed that nostalgic views of the past are encouraged by the increasing dominance of the visual image in the present. He suggests that 'there's a tendency to live, more and more, in a world of vivid, lurid immediacy, a present tense made more tense by the magnifying glass of the media. A present so powerful that it obliterates the past. That's simply something to be plundered for counterfeit nostalgia – its nothing but a quarry for pastiche music and "fashion". "Now" becomes NOW, a succession of overbright, hyped presents, more like sequins than sequence'.[17]

Echoing the arguments of Neil Postman,[18] Adams argues that the effects of our immersion in this overbright and lurid present has dire consequences for our abilities to engage in forms of public discourse that deal with the serious questions of the day, in religion, politics, the economy, education and the mass media. 'We are constantly confronted and astonished by events without precedent or context' claims Adams, 'yet imagine ourselves to be well-informed. That's how we buy tired, second-hand goods like the New Age or the New Right and imagine them to be revelations. Our lives are feverish, superficial and, for all our wondrous communications technologies, ignorant.'

This alleged shift from literacy to visualcy as the dominant means of communication in public discourse is closely associated with the postmodern turn in western societies.[19] It is something of an irony that so much currently fashionable writing on the topic of postmodernity, including writing on the 'postmodern body', fails to recognize that postmodernity along with modernity are temporal concepts, their application in social analysis requiring consideration of the relationships between past, present and future.

Along with this neglect of temporality in social analyses of the body has been a tendency of writers to remain silent on the question of the part schools and other educational institutions play in socially constructing bodies.[20] This absence of voice is particularly notable in relation to such activities in schools as sport, physical education, dance and manual arts, where one might have imagined there would be ample opportunity to observe such processes at work in starkly explicit forms.[21] Indeed, there is a considerable and long-standing stock of knowledge on how organized forms of physical activity might contribute to the better physiological, biomechanical and neurological functioning of children. Even though educational researchers have investigated how children's participation in organized physical activities contributes to inequities within the gender order, and various forms of social disadvantage,[22] the body somehow has been overlooked in these investigations. Perhaps this oversight is not surprising in the context of a culture that has accepted the body as a mainly biological phenomenon, regarding physical culture variously as mere play or mere physical activity. But this continuing absence of voice surely can no longer be justified given the centrality of educational practices to the social construction of bodies.

Anthropologist Marcel Mauss showed why educational practices are so central to this task in his discussion of the 'techniques of the body'. Mauss argued that the body is not a fixed biological category but is instead constituted by a variety of practices that both reflect and contribute to particular forms of social order. He cites differences in techniques of sleep, rest, care for the body, and movement, including different postures and gaits in walking and running, and different ways of dancing, jumping, climbing, descending, swimming and applying forceful movement.

In all of these elements of the art of using the human body, the facts of education were dominant. The notion of education could be superimposed on that of imitation. For there are particular children with very strong imitative faculties, others with very weak ones, but all of them go through the same education . . . What takes place is a prestigious imitation. The child, the adult, imitates actions which have succeeded and which he has seen successfully performed by people in whom he has confidence and who have authority over him.[23]

While Mauss's use of the term education extends beyond formally organized learning experiences in schools, his analysis of the techniques of the body demonstrates that our repertoires of movements, ranging from the everyday and commonplace to the specialized and complex, are learned activities. As such, they belong as much to the category of culture as nature. Mauss pointed out the extent to which learning techniques of the body are woven into the fabric of everyday life in all societies, and through his anthropological examples he demonstrated that learning, by virtue of its imitative nature, is a social process. He argued that techniques of the body differ within as well as across societies and that different stages of life are characterized by different forms of movement and bodily practices. Mauss showed that bodies are constructed 'not by [man] himself alone but by all his education, by the whole society to which he belongs, in the place he occupies in it';[24] in short, he shows that schooling bodies is constitutive of their social construction. Along with Mauss, Michel Foucault also understood that schools are sites in which bodies are constructed, in his terms through the diffusion of biopower. It is appropriate at this point to provide a sketch of some of the key ideas in Foucault's work that provide an underpinning framework for the arguments advanced in this book.

Biopower and Disciplinary Technology

In *Discipline and Punish*, Michel Foucault[25] noted that the school taking shape during the latter half of the nineteenth century was a key site for the regulation of bodies in space and in time alongside a diverse range of institutionalized social practices within, for instance, the family, the army, the new factories of the industrial revolution, and prisons. He developed the concept of 'disciplinary technology' to explain how this detailed attention to bodies instantiated new forms of what he called biopower.[26]

Biopower for Foucault is the integration of two forms of power over life, the first centred on the material body and its capabilities, the second focused on 'the species body'. The first form of power, an anatomo-politics of the human body, developed from the beginning of the seventeenth century, and the second, a biopolitics of population, began to emerge later, towards the end of the eighteenth century. It is towards the end of the nineteenth century that we find these two forms of biopower reaching a stage of close integration in a variety of institutions such as schools and through a range of specialized practices such as 'rational gymnastics'.[27] As competition in commerce among western nations intensified towards the end of the nineteenth century, we begin to see the question of population looming ever larger in public discourse and in the policies of governments.[28]

Disciplinary technology involved the diffusion of power throughout the social body, in contrast to the concentration of power in the body of the King. The social body and the body of the sovereign are abstract symbols of power. But use of these terms derives from the primacy of the actual, flesh-and-blood body in any system of social order. According to Foucault,[29] the body 'is directly involved in a political field; power relations have an immediate hold upon it; they invest it, mark it, train it, torture it, force it to carry out tasks, to perform ceremonies, to emit signs'. In capitalist societies, where economic productivity and wealth generation are at stake, the body must become productive and generative within the political field; 'the body becomes a useful force only if it is both a productive body and a subjective body'.[30] Individual liberty in the political sphere is forcefully counter-balanced by the needs of capital, such as compliant and appropriately skilled workers and consumers.

Foucault suggested that as disciplinary technology diffused through a range of social practices during the eighteenth and nineteenth centuries in Western Europe, new forms of corporeal power produced new knowledge. The possible domains of knowledge to which Foucault referred, the anatomo-metaphysical (in science and philosophy) and the technico-political (in military procedures, medicine, penal policy, and education), take the body as their central concern. The aim of each of these domains of knowledge was to know the body intimately and precisely in order to meet the dual purposes of productivity and compliance, or what Foucault called 'docility-utility', which were essential qualities of the urban citizenry in capitalist democracies. The outcome of specific and substantive power-knowledge combinations was not mere subjugation (as in slavery) but, rather, controlled production. In *Discipline and Punish*, Foucault usefully suggests these methods of knowing and controlling the body might be called disciplines; 'discipline produces subjected and practised bodies, docile bodies. Discipline increases the forces of the body (in economic terms of utility) and diminishes the same forces (in political terms of obedience).'[31]

Foucault's notion of docility-utility has a long lineage in educational practice. As Hoskins and Hamilton both note, docility is derived from the Latin *doceo*: I teach.[32] Hamilton suggested that in the sixteenth-century Scottish Calvinist text, *The Book of Discipline*, a docile child is a teachable child, someone who exhibits a readiness to learn.[33] Docility was a positive attribute, indicating a learner with intellectual promise. As the transformation from sovereignty to disciplinary society took place, and the technologies that constituted disciplinary society were diffused throughout the social body, the notion of docility came to mean something less dignified. In the nineteenth century, Hamilton claims that docility had come to suggest mere compliance, 'a person who had been tamed, if not accultured'. Against this prevailing view, Foucault argued that the work of schooling bodies was aimed at fostering compliance and productivity, suggesting a complex process that views school practices and public discourse as mutually constitutive.

Summarizing these insights of Foucault, Turner argued that four tasks relating to the body confronted western governments from the end of the eighteenth century: the reproduction of bodies over time, the regulation of bodies in space, the restraint of the inner body, and the representation of the outer body.[34] These tasks were interlinked. Given the prevalence of the view by the turn of the century that 'character is immanent in appearance',[35] that wholesomeness of personality and the inner self was displayed on the exterior surfaces of the body, any physical abnormality was a sure indication of some inner defect. The external appearance of normality was taken to be a mark of social worth, which for most working people was the capacity to play a designated, subordinate role in the wealth-making process.

Individual bodies were increasingly subject to intervention by western governments through the late eighteen and early nineteen hundreds in an attempt to regulate the reproduction and conduct of populations through increasing scrutiny, subjecting to the clinical gaze some of the most intimate and personal aspects of human life. According to Turner, the rise to prominence of modern medicine lay at the centre of a quest to know and thus to regulate both the individual and the social body. Linked in particular to the utilization of social surveys of diseased and 'defective' bodies, modern medicine was 'essentially social medicine as a policing of populations and a clinic of bodies'.[36]

School Practices

In using the notion of discipline to describe power–knowledge combinations aimed at producing compliant and yet productive bodies, Foucault was able to conflate the ideas of social regulation and knowledge and, in so doing, to provide a means of locating educational practices as one dimension of disciplinary technology that, together with other sets of 'little practices' within domains like the military, medicine and so on, made up the infrastructure of disciplinary society. Keith Hoskins[37] has shown that the examination, originating in the pedagogical practices of the universities of the twelfth century, was the wellspring of other forms of disciplinary technology developed to measure, record and relate in precise detail the nature of the body and its powers. The notion of disciplinary society itself, as Foucault used this term, rests on educational practices.[38]

The school practices that emerged during the latter part of the nineteenth century provide archetypal examples of disciplinary technology at work. As we saw in the case of Mr Carter's practices at Maryborough State School, the school operated as a differentiating space. In the classroom, differentiation was evident in the spatial distribution of pupils, allowing close supervision by the teacher. The seating of pupils in rows also made visible a hierarchy of competence and worth depending on where pupils were positioned in relation to the teacher and to each other. Disciplinary time combined with this attention to the differentiation of space to control the ebb and flow of the school day, the timetable specifying the precise periods of time to be spent on particular activities and ordering the sequence of work.

Within this form of schooling that took children's bodies as its subject matter, there emerged several sets of practices that had a specific and specialized relationship to schooling bodies: physical training, medical inspection and sport. Physical training for working-class boys and girls initially drew heavily on military drill and exercises from one or more of the systems that proliferated towards the end of the nineteenth century, most often the Ling system, only to give way to the less precise and exact performance of exercises between the First and Second World Wars and the addition of other activities such as swimming, rhythmic exercises and some minor games. In addition, it was not uncommon to find purely military activities such as squad and rifle drilling as cadet training in the schools for privileged boys.

Together with school medical inspection, early forms of physical training best exemplify the processes of corporeal regulation illustrated by Mr Carter's school assembly. Medical inspection, which was often coupled with this drilling and exercising form of physical training in educational policy prior to the 1940s, was particularly prominent in schools in most Australian states for over forty years. Until the beginning of the Second World War, these practices were concerned principally with the meticulous measurement of children's bodies, when the medical inspectors' relocation to departments of health services from departments of education required a shift in priorities and a need to work on tasks of a different order.

Sport, initially the province of males and some females of the privileged classes, later became established as an extracurricular activity for boys and girls in most government schools, though the sports that were played often differed greatly depending on social class and the sex of the pupil. While sport, particularly competitive team games, appear to offer a counterpoint to the regimentation and precision of physical training and meticulous attention to detail of medical inspection, this practice was nevertheless just as concerned with the regulation of bodies in space and in time and might be viewed in Foucault's terms as a 'looser form of power' over the body. These regulative imperatives in sport are immediately apparent in the ways in which the rules of games require bodies to perform within strictly defined parameters. We might add to this the pervasive influence of the games ethic, originating in the schools of the privileged classes to become a significant force in shaping practices in government schools by the end of the Second World War, which constituted a powerful moral code for proper heterosexual masculine and feminine conduct.

The core business of each of these sets of practices was the regulation and normalization of children's bodies, and each demonstrated a shared concern for meticulous, detailed and precise work on the body that characterized other forms of disciplinary technology. Taken together, these three interlocking sets of activities formed a complex matrix of discursive practices that had as their special responsibility the schooling of bodies. The forms that these regulative techniques took depended to a great extent on the socio-economic location of the school in which they were practised and on the sex and race of the children who were their subjects.

In addition to their operation as technologies of power, each set of practices can be viewed as part of what Foucault referred to as the incitement to discourse on sexuality and progeniture. Foucault suggested that the verbalization and codification of sexuality in particular fields of knowledge, such as medicine, child care and psychoanalysis, was a preoccupation of the bourgeoisie and was a central aspect in the formation of their class identity. Just as the aristocracy had marked off its exclusiveness on the basis of blood-lines, so the bourgeoisie attempted to establish its distinctive class identity and location on the basis of 'its progeny and the health of its organism'.[39] By the late 1800s, after the bourgeoisie's social locations within the industrial order had been more fully developed, these class-specific concerns began to be articulated as national concerns, as matters of vital importance to the race and the Nation State. Dreyfus and Rabinow remark that 'once the sexualisation of individuals and populations had spread through the society, the differentiating mark of class could no longer be the bourgeois preoccupation with sexuality. Sex as meaning now expands to sex as administrative control.'[40] It was from within the various strata of the bourgeoisie, particularly among professionals, public servants and scientists, that advocacy for the application of practices such as physical training, medical inspection and sport came, not from the masses who by and large had become the objects of these practices. These school practices can thus be seen as key components of the bourgeois incitement to discourse on sexuality and a means of regulating and normalizing children's bodies. Each of these sets of school practices was embedded in public discourse that provided the raw materials for their construction as meaningful activities.

Public Discourse

In Australia, the school practices of physical training, medical inspection and sport were profoundly shaped by a quest for nationhood that followed federation in 1901. Both in these conditions and in the forms of school activities they constructed, we can see the workings of biopower, focused on the individualized, objectified moving body, as Australians attempted to forge an economically productive nation and a national identity out of parochialism, cultural difference and a colonial mentality. Concerns for the physical deterioration of the Anglo-Celtic race drew heavily on widespread public discussion on this issue in Britain and on the discourse of eugenics. Physical training, medical inspection and sport, as part of the institution of schooling, were deeply implicated in this process, demonstrating intricate and detailed attention to working on the bodies of children, to their correct deportment and to their productive deployment.

Federation and the quest for nationhood

Questions surrounding nationhood and race occupied some significant space in public discourse in the period leading up to and following federation. Conversations around and about these topics generated ideas and values which were manifest in the workings of a range of social institutions, particularly those representing the military and national defence, health and education. But their reach went far beyond these spheres of life. Questions of what it was to be an Australian were never far from the surface of public debates over the economy and wealth, religion, politics and power, and of course, the relationship with Britain. Such questions were not confined to the statements of politicians or intellectuals. People in everyday life could not avoid regularly meeting and engaging in some way the question 'Who are We?'[41]

This is not to suggest that there was any uniform interest in this question among the five million or so people who inhabited Australia by 1914, nor a consistent nor even coherent response.[42] The question was problematic and riddled with tensions and contradictions. At the same time, these tensions did little to disrupt the social and economic order of Australian society in the period leading up to 1914.[43] This relative stability existed despite the depression of the 1890s and the long drought which compounded its effects in southern and eastern states until 1903, almost fatally wounding the former confidence many people had had in the benign and bountiful

Australian environment.[44] It was Australia's involvement in the First World War, the great sacrifices that had to be made both at home and in Europe, which finally brought to the surface many of the resentments, hatreds, jealousies, rivalries, and conflicts that had been simmering and brewing before the processes leading to federation were set in train in the early 1890s.[45] Issues relating to nationalism and race were integral to most of the conflicts that erupted during the war years and which at times even threatened to bring a premature end to the Commonwealth of Australia.

The push towards federation in the 1890s was borne out of economic necessity, concerns over the territorial ambitions of France, Russia and Japan and, according to Manning Clark,[46] an almost hysterical fear of the coloured workforce among white Australians. When federation was finally achieved in 1901, the new Commonwealth government presided over a nation in name only. Parochialism and inter-state jealousies were deeply seated, all the more so since they were closely tied to economic interests, jurisdiction and power. Within the pre-federation colonies, especially during the early 1890s and the depression, those selected to draw up the constitution were viewed suspiciously by workers' representatives as members of a bourgeois conspiracy.[47] Meanwhile, throughout this period, the Irish were increasingly pushed to the margins of respectable society, forming a substantial white underclass because of their Catholicism and their anti-capitalist politics. And then there was the struggle for the universal franchise which, though a concern of the better educated and wealthier women in the main, was finally achieved by 1903 for Commonwealth elections and by 1909 for all states. Even among the makers of wealth and profit, there were divergent interests that were difficult to reconcile without acrimony.[48]

Against this backdrop of parochialism, racial, class and religious conflict and women's suffrage, it is hardly surprising that several Prime Ministers and their governments attempted to foreground the issue of national identity. But their attempts to reconcile so many social and cultural differences simply served to reveal the apparently intractable nature of the problems facing the new nation. In 1901, according to Alfred Deakin, the problem of coloured labour touched

> the profoundest instinct of individual or nation – the instinct of self-preservation – for it is nothing less than the national manhood, the national character, and the national future that are at stake . . . . No motive power operated more universally . . . and more powerfully in dissolving the technical and arbitrary political divisions which previously separated us than did the desire that we should be one people and remain one people without the admixture of other races.[49]

17

This type of thinking, widely shared among the Anglo-Celtic community, suggested that to be Australian was to be white, and it lead in 1905 to a general acceptance of the so-called White Australia Policy as the basis for population planning. Aboriginals were excluded from official population counts and from consideration as Australian citizens.[50] The notion of an Anglo-Celtic race in the southern hemisphere, cut adrift from its history and heritage, was the source of further terrors. The defence of a white Australia raised the question of Australia's relationship with Britain, and was little source of comfort. The difficulties were both constitutional and cultural. The head of state was a British monarch, and the national anthem was 'God Save the King'. Yet, when Australian concerns touched on Britain's economic interests, the British saw little need to make concessions that might broaden Australia's limited sovereignty.[51]

The ties of sentiment were potentially even more damaging to the realization of Australian nationhood. Their shared British heritage was a touchstone that linked the otherwise parochial colonies, and which set the standard for civilized society in what was often a hostile and foreign environment. At the same time, the strong identification of many Australians with all things British jarred with equally strongly held Republican sentiments. The schizophrenic nature of Australian nationalism was well demonstrated by the many who thought of themselves as 'Independent Australian Britons'.[52] Yet, over the forty-year period between 1861 and 1901, the percentage of the population born in the Australian colonies had risen sharply from just over 50 per cent to 82 per cent.[53] It was among the wealthy, the socially ambitious and the powerful that sentiment for the 'Old Country' was strongest, and it was to Britain that Australia's elites looked constantly for confirmation of the benchmarks of social status and exclusiveness. The establishment of Empire Day in 1905 by the Conservative Prime Minister George Reid was a case in point, an initiative that was intended to mobilize public support for the British Empire, and that was especially targeted at schools. In the process, the establishment of Empire Day managed to promote discord among the Catholics due to its Anglophile overtones, and among the Nationalists due to Reid's concerns to link the celebration of Empire to his anti-socialist crusade.[54]

The many privileged young men who rushed to defend the Empire 'in a haze of Anglophile emotion'[55] at the outbreak of hostilities in 1914 was another example of this Anglomania, while ordinary Australians showed less zeal to fight, with around only two-fifths of men of military age enlisting. The war itself was to figure large in the quest for nationhood, though as much through disillusionment with Britain as through any positive assertion of distinctively Australian characteristics. We should note that the conduct of Australian troops throughout the war earned them a reputation for courage, doggedness and exceptional camaraderie, and also for insubordination, intolerance and general larrikinism. And politician William Hughes was quick during postwar reparations to capitalize on the legend Gallipoli was to become, claiming that Australia earned nationhood through its contribution to the war which cost some 59,000 dead and 167,000 wounded, about two-thirds of the total number who enlisted.[56] But despite the mythologies of Australian nationhood the war generated, one of the more bitter memories, particularly for the Anglophile elites, was Britain's ingratitude for Australia's contribution to the defence of her Empire, ingratitude that stung all the more sharply since the survival of a white race in the southern hemisphere was itself in question.

Eugenics and the 'Future Australian Race'

The preoccupation with nationhood and racial purity during this period were by no means peculiar to Australia. Along with the great movements of populations from rural to urban centres within industrialized countries, and the successive waves of immigration throughout the nineteenth century following earlier colonization, came fears for continuing 'supremacy' and 'integrity' of the white races. In the United States and Britain, eugenicists argued that the 'unfit', physical and mental defectives and the poor, were out-breeding the 'fit'. Leading eugenicists in the USA, among them eminent physicians and psychologists such as Coleman and Jencks, argued that the coloured races were diluting and contaminating the Anglo-Celtic stock, and they advocated compulsory sterilization of black defectives who, they suggested, could be identified through the administration of IQ tests.[57] In Europe and America, informed opinion came down on the side of hereditary factors over the environment in determining the likelihood of propagation of defective genes. In contrast, during the first two decades of the twentieth century Australian eugenicists manipulated the available evidence to demonstrate the benign and wholesome nature of the Australian environment in overcoming race degeneration.

Emerging from the economic depression of the 1890s, the average Australian's faith in the bountifulness of the Australian environment was shaken, but not completely undermined.[58] In the reformist zeal that led the recovery, questions of the fitness of the population and national prosperity seemed to go hand in hand. Schools were targeted as important sites for reformist action in relation to both issues, and an early formulation of human capital theory began to emerge in the form of advocacy for government-sponsored technical education for 'national efficiency'.[59] Germany's manufacturing productivity had a number of often grudging admirers in Australia and Britain, who saw German technical and vocational education as the key to its success in the economic sphere. In all of these discussions

19

of national efficiency, the themes of economic success, race degeneration and the health and fitness of the population intertwined.

It was within this context that eugenicists' ideas about hereditary and environmental influences on racial purity and degeneracy began to receive widespread attention from members of the professional classes, particularly within the scientific, public health and education communities.[60] Eugenics represented a serious and concerted effort to apply the laws of heredity to the control of human propagation and so to retain only those inborn qualities possessed by those considered to be the more productive and socially adept members of society. While the production of populations over time was the central focus of eugenics, the concern to determine which characteristics were inherited and which were acquired lead Australian eugenicists to debate the relative contributions of nature over nurture.

Darwin's revelation that humans were part of the organic world and his hypothesis of natural selection raised the possibility for many people that human beings might learn to control their own evolution. Breakthroughs in understanding human genetics towards the turn of the nineteenth century fuelled this hope. However, Mark Haller has suggested that the early eugenicists 'greatly oversimplified the problem of human genetics'.[61] Many others who were attracted by the implications of eugenics for social improvement would have agreed, since they did not necessarily accept as given the proposition that heredity had an overriding role in determining racial characteristics. Consequently, they set about investigating the relative contributions of heredity and environment to the production of human defects.

At least two major orientations to eugenics emerged from these tensions. In positive eugenics, the optimistic view was held that while heredity played an incontrovertible role in determining the evolutionary process it was possible to intervene in this process by manipulation of the environment, usually through medical, public health or educational practices. In negative eugenics, a more pessimistic view held that control of the breeding of people already identified as defective, either physically, mentally or morally, usually through sterilization and selective breeding, were the main means of regulating human propagation in a desired direction.[62]

Caroline Bacchi argued that, in contrast to European and American eugenicists, the idea was widespread in Australia before 1914 that 'state action could remove the causes of class hostility and create a new and healthy social order. A program of progressive social legislation logically necessitated a belief in the benefits of "nurture"'.[63] Mary Cawte suggested that Bacchi rather overstates this environmentalist stance and that forms of hereditarian determinism championed by the likes of R.J.A. Berry were at least as influential as environmentalism in Australia.[64] Stephen Garton has likewise proposed that, following the First World War, eugenics began to have a greater influence on public policy as reformers became more accepting of the solutions presented by negative eugenics, including sterilization of the mentally and physically disabled.[65]

The discussions of each of these historians suggests that faith in the potentially benign effects of the environment among Australian eugenicists did not amount to a rejection of the influence of heredity so much as a privileging of nurture over nature. As Bacchi concluded, the environmentalists suffered a declining faith during the conservative interwar years, with the apparently increasing 'menace of the feeble-minded' winning many converts to hereditary determinism. At the same time, she identified an important stream of Australian sentiment up until the First World War with regard to interventionist attempts at social regulation in which gaining control of the environment and turning it to industrially and socially productive use was of central concern.

The Antipodean environment was considered to be rich in natural resources but also, as Bacchi noted, it was thought of as a frontier. As such, colonial Australia was perceived to possess a wildness that had in some way to be overcome and if not tamed or subdued then at least rendered harmless to the Anglo-Celt. More positively, many Australian eugenicists and others sympathetic to eugenic ideals believed great benefits to racial development would ensue if the more wholesome aspects of this foreign environment could be harnessed to the cause of social progress. While Bacchi and Garton point out that there was no specific eugenic legislation enacted in Australia prior to 1913, the idea that the Australian race-type might be improved through careful monitoring of the effects of the environment on the Anglo-Celtic stock through such strategies as anthropometry[66] which could feed a range of social, educational and medical policies and practices had widespread support which intensified in the period leading up to the First World War.

Interest in the question of the effects of the climate and other environmental factors on the Australian race-type had gathered pace in the second half of the nineteenth century. Marcus Clarke's monograph *The Future Australian Race*[67] which appeared in 1877, demonstrated a strong allegiance to Darwin's ideas on evolution and laid out a detailed discussion of the ways in which the Anglo-Celtic stock would undergo progressive adaptations to the Australian environment. North of a line drawn through the centre of the continent 'will evolve a luxurious and stupendous civilisation only removed from that of Egypt and Mexico by the measure of remembrance of European democracy' while beneath this line 'will be a Republic, having the mean climate, and, in comparison, the development of Greece'. These contrasting climates will not only breed different political cultures, according to Clarke, but will also shape the personalities and the physical features of future Australasians. 'The sun beating on the face closes the eyes, puckers the cheeks, and contracts the muscles of the orbit. Our children will have deep-set eyes with over-hanging brows . . . the custom of meat eating will square the jaw and render the hair coarse but plentiful. The Australasian will be a square-headed, masterful man, with full temples, plenty of beard, a keen eye, a stern and yet sensual mouth. His teeth will be bad and his lungs good. He will suffer from liver disease, and become prematurely bald.' These speculations by Clarke may have been rather fanciful, and they were quite clearly sexist and also racist, in so far as they discounted entirely the indigenous population as an example of human adaptation to the Australian environment. But they nevertheless reflected formative undercurrents of sentiment in a new country self-consciously seeking a national identity.

Dr Philip Muskett's book, *The Diet of Australian School Children*,[68] published in 1899, is a case in point. A former Senior Resident Medical Officer at the Sydney Hospital, Muskett confidently predicted that 'technical education can help to bring about, in all the Australias, continuous and ever-widening progress, commercial expansion, and industrial activity'. As a Nationalist, Muskett was extremely interested in arguments about the Australian race-type and took a firm environmentalist stance, stating that until the Anglo-Celtic race came to terms with the semi-tropical climate of Australia, no distinctive breed could emerge. Linked to his arguments for emulating the German example of vocational technical education, he suggested that 'if Australia is to be inhabited by a healthy and vigorous people, there must be more attention paid to physical health. The continuity of a robust race can only be secured by the perpetuation of a sound stock . . . there is a great competition in the world of to-day, and the weakest go to the wall faster than he ever did before.'

In this competitive environment where only the fittest survived, the declining birth rate among sections of the white Australian population generated widespread concern, a matter which was central to Foucault's positioning concerns for the propagation of populations over time as one of the four components of biopower. At the turn of the century, T.A. Coghlan,[69] a New South Wales government statistician, revealed that the crude birth rate had dropped from 35 per thousand in 1890 to 25 per thousand in 1900. Moreover, it was among the ruling and socially aspiring classes that the falls had been greatest due to the growing practice of birth control, a matter which had prompted some Americans to argue that Anglo-Celts were engaging in race suicide.[70] Coghlan's findings lead directly to the establishment of the Birth Rate Commission in 1903 and followed the lead of a British Interdepartmental Committee on the birth rate that had reported the year before.[71] The Commissioners initially considered calls to ban contraception, but pressure from a number of sources caused them to reconsider this course of action. In the same year Coghlan's findings were reported, the Australian baby health movement was formed.

Writing retrospectively in 1939, one of its leading members, W.G. Armstrong,[72] was able to report that between 1903–14, the infant mortality rate had dropped from 167 to 68 per thousand live births. Both Armstrong and Coghlan among others were firm supporters of education and medical inspection as forms of intervention and as key strategies of prevention. It was these strategies, not stricter controls on the importation of contraceptives and abortifacients initially favoured by the Birth Rate Commissioners, which brought about this reduction in infant mortality. In his 1902 presidential address to the Australasian Association for the Advancement of Science, Coghlan outlined the case for anthropometric measurements of children as a means of informing educational and medical practices.

> In most countries a fair share of attention has been devoted to the measurement of adults, but the chief attention is being paid to children. This is as it should be, for the measurement of children is of the utmost importance, because here we are closest to the source of social and national life. The mental and physical defects and abnormalities of the child we may hope to counteract or remove, whereas similar shortcomings and peculiarities of the adult are beyond remedy. The object of all worthy educational systems is the freest and most symmetrical development of individual minds and bodies, and the training of our future citizens so they may approximate, as nearly as possible, the ideal human type.[73]

On the basis of this kind of argument, the Birth Rate Commissioners eventually concluded that control of infant mortality would be a more effective solution to the problem. One of their recommendations was that there should be regular medical inspections of school children. This recommendation echoed a major outcome of the Royal Commission on Physical Training in Britain, set up in 1902 following agitation by a militarist lobby to institute military drill in British government schools, but shifting its focus during the sitting to the physical, environmental and social welfare of children.[74] Despite this early British precedent and the support of the Birth Rate Commissioners, regular medical inspections were not instituted by state governments in Australia until the British had established school medical services following investigations of a second Royal Commission on Physical Deterioration which reported in 1904.

Bacchi argued that by 1905 public opinion had swung around completely from questions of birth control to concerns for child welfare and health instruction for mothers and children. The work of the baby health movement and this shift in focus to child welfare offered strong support to Australian eugenicists' views that environmental factors played a significant part in preventing or overcoming defective characteristics. Behind the statistical evidence presented by Coghlan and others lay a conviction resting on faith that the bountiful and benign qualities of the Australian environment, which many social reformers considered offered a distinct advantage over the ills of the Old World, could develop a hardy, healthy and productive race of Anglo-Celts in the southern hemisphere. According to Bacchi, 'environmentalism provided hope for the future. Hereditary determinism seemed fatalistic, particularly in Australia, given her convict heritage'.[75]

From the end of the nineteenth century until the onset of the First World War, it was mainly positive eugenics that attracted the attention of Australians in the fields of science, education, medicine and public health. In these concerns for the fitness of the Anglo-Celtic race and economic productivity, it is clearly evident that the propagation of the population in time and its control in space has been an underwriting concern in the construction of Australian society, particularly in this formative phase leading up to and following federation. The attempt to school bodies needs to be viewed as a constituent part of this process. The extraordinarily precise and meticulous attention to the detail of schooling bodies shown in physical training and school medical inspection in particular attests to the concern not merely to control children's bodies, but to harness their energies to the pursuit of economic prosperity. These school practices can in this context be viewed as micro-technologies of power, aimed at ordering the body and harnessing its forces in time and space.

Schooling Bodies, School Practice, Public Discourse

This book undertakes a detailed and sustained historical investigation of the emergence, consolidation and reconstruction of the school practices of physical training, medical inspection and sport between the 1880s and the 1940s with the principal aim of demonstrating how these processes have contributed to schooling bodies. The book illustrates some of the ways in which these school practices have been both participants in and outcomes of the processes of constructing and constituting the body in modernity, and makes the claim that shifts in these practices' treatment of the body during this century are indicative of shifts in public discourse and biopower more broadly.

Foucault captures something of the nature of these shifts in his suggestion that social regulation of the body in the mid to late twentieth century has been accomplished through distinctively different processes than was the case during the preceding two centuries. He argued that 'from the eighteenth century to the early twentieth century I think it was believed that the investment of the body by power had to be heavy, ponderous, meticulous and constant . . . And then, starting from the 1960s, it began to be realised that such a cumbersome form of power was no longer as indispensable as had been thought and that industrial societies could content themselves with a looser form of power over the body'.[76] Although I will challenge his dating of this process, Foucault's characterization of this shift in the manner of normalization and regulation of the body offers a useful focus for the argument to be pursued in this book, since it is suggestive of a body in contemporary society that is regulated less coercively and externally by others and more often internally, by the self. The shift to a looser form of corporeal power suggests an associated shift in the locus of regulation, from external and mass practices to internal and individual practices.

The changing forms of schooling bodies explored in this book provide an opportunity to examine some dimensions of the individualization, internalization and diffusion of biopower in the first half of this century. My argument, in summary, is that the emergence of practices of schooling bodies since the late 1800s is closely associated with the construction of the body within a phase of modernity Foucault describes as disciplinary society, informed by the notions that the body can be both disciplined and energized through mass educational, medical, and other interventions to be economically productive and politically acquiescent. I will suggest that by the end of the Second World War a notable shift had taken place in the form of corporeal regulation from a regimented, precise and meticulous form to a looser form of power over the body, moving towards the individualization, internalization and diffusion of biopower. The next chapter begins the process of substantiating this argument by examining the emergence and consolidation of militarized practices of drilling bodies that were aimed explicitly at regulating children's bodies.

Notes and References

1 Education Department of Victoria (1903) *Education Gazette and Teachers' Aid* Melbourne: Government Printer, p. 31.
2 *Education Gazette and Teachers' Aid*, p. 32.
3 Foucault, M. (1977) *Discipline and Punish* New York: Allen & Unwin, p. 143.
4 Davison, G. (1993) *The Unforgiving Minute: How Australia Learned to Tell the Time* Melbourne: Oxford University Press, p. 5.
5 Corrigan, P. (1988) The making of the boy: meditations on what grammar school did with, to, and for my body *Journal of Education*, **170** (3), pp. 142–61.
6 Corrigan, The making of the boy.
7 Techow, G. (1866) *Manual of Gymnastic Exercises for the Use of Schools and at Home* Melbourne, p. xii.
8 Techow, *Manual of Gymnastic Exercises*, pp. 3–4.
9 McIntosh, P.C. (1968) *Physical Education in England Since 1800* London: Bell, 2nd edn; Munrow, A.D. (1955) *Pure and Applied Gymnastics* London: Arnold.
10 Techow, *Manual of Gymnastic Exercises*, p. xii.

11 Franks, A.W. (1990) Bringing bodies back in: a decade review *Theory, Culture and Society*, **7**, pp. 131–62; Cranny-Francis, A. (1995) *The Body as Text* Carlton: Melbourne University Press.
12 Fitzclarence, L. (1990) The body as commodity, in Rowe, D. and Lawrence, G. (eds) *Sport and Leisure: Trends in Australian Popular Culture* Sydney: Harcourt Brace Jovanovich, pp. 96–108; Grosz, E. (1994) *Volatile Bodies: Towards a Corporeal Feminism* Sydney: Allen & Unwin; Cranny-Francis, *The Body as Text*.
13 Shilling, C. (1993) *The Body and Social Theory* London: Sage, p. 204.
14 Some notable exceptions to this omission are Foucault (1977) *Discipline and Punish*; Turner, B.S. (1992) *Regulating Bodies: Essays in Medical Sociology* London: Routledge; and Dutton, K. (1995) *The Perfectible Body: The Western Ideal of Physical Development* London: Cassell.
15 Lowenthal, D. (1985) *The Past is a Foreign Country* Cambridge: Cambridge University Press, p. 4.
16 Nauright, J. (1995) Rugby and the nostalgia of masculinity in New Zealand and South Africa *Journal of Comparative Physical Education and Sport*, **17** (1), pp. 24–34.
17 Adams, P. (1989) in *The Weekend Australian Review*, 19–20 August, p. 2.
18 Postman, N. (1985) *Amusing Ourselves to Death: Public Discourse in the Age of Show Business* London: Heinneman.
19 Lyotard, J-F. (1984) *The Post-Modern Condition* Minneapolis: University of Minnesota Press; Harvey, D. (1989) *The Condition of Postmodernity* Oxford: Blackwell.
20 Exceptions include Corrigan, The making of the boy; McLaren, P. (1988) Schooling the postmodern body: critical pedagogy and the politics of enfleshment *Journal of Education*, **170** (3), pp. 53–83; Shilling, C. (1991) Educating the body: physical capital and the production of social inequalities *Sociology*, **25** (4), pp. 653–72; Connell, R.W. (1989) Cool guys, swots and wimps: the interplay of masculinity and education *The Oxford Review of Education*, **15** (3), pp. 291–303.
21 One of the few exceptions is Hargreaves, J. (1986) *Sport, Power and Culture* Cambridge: Polity.
22 One exception here is the work of Jan Wright, e.g. Wright, J. (1997) A feminist poststructuralist methodology for the study of gender construction in physical education: description of a study *Journal of Teaching in Physical Education*, **15** (1), pp. 1–24; and Kirk, D. and Wright, J. (1995) The social construction of bodies: implications for the health and physical education curriculum *Unicorn*, **21** (4), pp. 63–73.
23 Mauss, M. (1973) Techniques of the body *Economy and Society*, **2**, pp. 70–87, (Trans. B. Brewster).
24 Mauss, Techniques of the body, p. 76
25 Foucault, *Discipline and Punish*.
26 Foucault, M. (1984) *The History of Sexuality: An Introduction* Harmondsworth: Penguin, pp. 140–44.
27 Broekhoff, J. (1972) Physical education and the reification of the human body *Gymnasion*, **9**, pp. 4–11.
28 Lewis, M. (1988) The 'Health of the Race' and infant health in New South Wales: perspectives on medicine and empire, in Macleod, E. and Lewis, M. (eds) *Disease, Medicine and Empire: Perspecitves on Western Medicine and the Experience of European Expansion* London: Routledge. .

29 Foucault, *Discipline and Punish*, pp. 25–6.
30 Foucault, *Discipline and Punish*, p. 28.
31 Foucault, *Discipline and Punish*, p. 138.
32 Hamilton, D. (1991) *Learning About Education* Milton Keynes: Open University Press; Hoskins, K. (1990) Foucault under examination: the crypto-educationalist unmasked, in Ball, S.J. (ed.) *Foucault and Education* London: Routledge, pp. 29–56.
33 See John Knox in Boyd, W. and King, E.J. (1975) *The History of Western Education* London: Adam and Charles Black, 11th edn, p. 202.
34 Turner, *The Body and Society*.
35 Finkelstein, J. (1991) *The Fashioned Self* Cambridge: Polity Press.
36 Turner, *The Body and Society*, p. 50.
37 Hoskins, Foucault under examination.
38 Cf. Luke, C. (1989) *Pedagogy, Printing and Protestantism: The Discourse on Childhood* Albany, NY: State University of New York Press.
39 Foucault, *The History of Sexuality*, p. 124.
40 Dreyfus, H. and Rabinow, P. (1982) *Michel Foucault: Beyond Structuralism and Hermeneutics* Brighton: The Harvester Press, p. 141.
41 See Clark, Marcus (1877) *The Future Australian Race* Melbourne: A.H. Massina & Co. for an early discussion.
42 Macintyre, S. (1993) *The Oxford History of Australia (Volume 4) 1901–1942* Melbourne: Oxford University Press, p. 123.
43 Clark, Manning (1981) *A Short History of Australia* Sydney: Mead & Beckett (Illustrated 2nd edn), p. 156.
44 Blainey, G. (1980) *A Land Half Won* Melbourne: Macmillan.
45 McKernan, M. (1979) Sport, war and society: Australia, 1914–1918, in Cashman, R. and McKernan, M. (eds) *Sport in History* St. Lucia: University of Queensland Press, pp. 1–20.
46 Clark, *A Short History of Australia*, p. 163.
47 Clark, *A Short History of Australia*, p. 166.
48 Macintyre, *The Oxford History*, p. 191.
49 In Clark, *A Short History of Australia*, p. 163.
50 Macintyre, *The Oxford History*, p. 34 and p. 124.
51 Macintyre, *The Oxford History*, pp. 126–7.
52 Macintyre, *The Oxford History*, p. 23
53 Clark, *A Short History of Australia*, p. 145.
54 Macintyre, *The Oxford History*, pp. 132–3.
55 Macintyre, *The Oxford History*, pp. 180–1.
56 Macintyre, *The Oxford History*, p. 177.
57 Kamin, L.J. (1977) *The Science and Politics of I.Q.* Harmondsworth: Penguin; Gould, S.J. (1981) *The Mismeasure of Man* New York: Norton.
58 Blainey, *A Land Half Won*.
59 Connell, W.F. (1980) *A History of Education in the Twentieth Century* Canberra: CDC.
60 Searle, G.R. (1976) *Eugenics and Politics in Britain 1900–1914* Leyden: Noordhoff; Weindling, P. (1989) *Health, Race and German Politics between National Unification and Nazism 1870–1945* Cambridge: Cambridge University Press.

61 Haller, M.H. (1963) *Eugenics: Heriditarian Attitudes in American Thought* New Brunswick, NJ: Rutgers University Press.

62 Searle, *Eugenics and Politics in Britain*, Chapters 7 and 8.

63 Bacchi, C. (1980) The nature–nurture debate in Australia, 1900–1914 *Historical Studies*, **19** (5), p. 200.

64 Cawte, M. (1986) Craniometry and eugenics in Australia: R.J.A. Berry and the quest for social efficiency *Historical Studies*, **22** (6), pp. 35–53.

65 Garton, S. (1986) Sir Charles Mackellar: psychiatry, eugenics and child welfare in New South Wales, 1900–1914 *Historical Studies*, **22** (6), pp. 21–34.

66 Anthropometry, 'the exact measurement of the anatomical, physiological and psychological characters of man', provides an insight into the ways in which questions of racial degeneration and the emerging Australian race-type were posed within the fields of preventative medicine, public health and compulsory mass education, and also exemplifies Foucault's emphasis on the little practices of biopower which were concerned with the examination of bodies in precise detail. See Booth, M. (1911) School anthropometrics, Australasian Association for the Advancement of Science *AAAS Conference Proceedings*, p. 689.

67 Clarke, *The Future Australian Race*, pp. 20–2.

68 Muskett, P.E. (1899) *The Diet of Australian School Children (with also health and disease during school life), and Technical Education* Melbourne: George Robertson, p. 149.

69 Coghlan, T.A. (1903) *The Decline of the Birth-Rate in New South Wales* Sydney: W.A. Gullick, Government Printer.

70 Lewis, The 'Health of the Race', p. 303.

71 Coghlan, *The Decline of the Birth-Rate*.

72 Armstrong, W.G. (1939) The beginnings of Baby Health Centres in New South Wales *Medical Journal of Australia*, p. 672.

73 Coghlan, T.A. (1902) Child measurement, *AAAS Conference Proceedings*, pp. 542–3.

74 Thompson, I. (1978) The origins of Physical Education in State Schools *Scottish Educational Review*, **10** (2), pp. 17–34.

75 Bacchi, The nature–nurture debate, p. 200.

76 Foucault, M. (1980) *Power/Knowledge: Selected Interviews and Other Writings* Brighton: Harvester Press, p. 58 (Trans. C. Gordon).

2

Drilling Bodies: The Emergence of Militarized Physical Training

The disciplinary value of drill was everywhere recognised, for it seemed the only way of assembling large numbers of children in restricted spaces, and of moving them safely from one part of a school to another . . . . In the early years of the schools, particularly when compulsory attendance was enforced by the prosecution of recalcitrant parents, the free use of corporal punishment and a rigid code of external discipline seemed the only possible means of quelling ill-disciplined and even riotous children.[1]

The introduction of compulsory mass schooling in Australia during the final two decades of the nineteenth century, and a decade or so earlier in Britain, presented schools and their teachers with the major challenge of establishing order, control and discipline among their pupils. Before even the most elementary learning of the rudiments of reading, writing and arithmetic might commence, pupils needed to be rendered receptive to instruction through the imposition of order, with the result that corporal punishment in the form of the leather tawse or the cane was freely and frequently used in schools, in the colonial schools of Australia on both boys and girls as young as five years of age.[2]

While this formalized and officially sanctioned violence was a favoured means of establishing order and obedience among children, school authorities were quick to recognize the resentment physical punishment created among its victims and its relative ineffectiveness in controlling the wayward behaviour of the most recalcitrant of pupils. It is not surprising that, in attempting to confront the problem of order, schools turned to the already well-established and demonstrably effective practices used by the military for controlling large numbers of soldiers. Military practices represented a ready-made technology of power well suited to the manipulation of potentially unruly bodies in space and in time, and they offered schools a stock of physical activities and scripts containing words of command and advice on how these activities should be implemented. Militarists also saw great benefit in using schools as a training ground for soldiers of the future and in both Australia and Britain they were well placed and numerous enough to constitute a powerful, if not always successful, lobby group.

The efficacy of military practices in establishing order and discipline in the new mass elementary schools seemed transparent to school administrators and highly convenient to militarists. However, almost as soon as these practices were implemented social reformers began to question whether this approach to schooling bodies might be preventing children from taking advantage of instruction rather than assisting them. As early as 1883 in Britain, concerns were expressed that drilling children who were malnourished, disabled or in poor health was a form of 'over-pressure' that was likely to contribute to their further physical deterioration.[3] Shock at the defeats suffered by the British army during the Boer War, which ended in 1902, resonated throughout the Empire and was so keenly felt that the public were forced to attend to a mass of information accumulated by social reformers during the previous thirty years on the serious health problems experienced by the urban poor in Britain.[4] In a chain reaction, ongoing investigations of public health issues in Australia were given legitimation through this process.[5]

By the turn of the century, debates in both countries concerning the form physical training should take in schools swung around the poles of militarism and public health. The Royal Commission on Physical Training, ostensibly concerned only with Scotland, had a highly significant impact on the development of school medical services in the rest of Britain and in Australia when it reported in 1903, and in the process signalled the ascendancy of the public health lobby, the emergence of the school as a site for medical interventions, and the development of what was intended to be a therapeutic form of physical training. As we will see, by the end of the first decade of the 1900s in Britain the militarist lobby was all but defeated in its plans for compulsory military training in schools. In contrast, and for once going against the precedent set by Britain, Australia's decision-makers elected to institute a scheme of compulsory junior cadet training for schoolboys aged twelve to fourteen based on a system of physical training that was also intended to suit girls and younger boys.

The poles of the debate may have been formed by the apparently competing philosophies of militarism and public health at the level of policy, but the aims of both were relatively easy to accommodate in school practice. This is because drilling and exercising and school medical inspection and anthropometry shared a common concern to regulate and normalize children's bodies. Each set of practices operated as a technology of power, utilizing precise, meticulous and systematic methods to train, examine and measure children's bodies. Militarism may have fallen from favour in Britain some twenty years before its official demise in Australia, but in both countries it exerted a profound and lasting influence on the conduct and substance of physical training. The aim of this chapter is to explore the emergence of the practices that sought to produce the drilled body in early mass elementary schools, a body schooled to move efficiently, productively and at all times obediently.

Drilling, Exercising and Social Order in Schools

In Australia, compulsory elementary schooling had been established in most of the colonies during the decade following the withdrawal of the British forces. Without standing armies of professional soldiers, the colonial governments saw schools as convenient training grounds for their volunteer citizen armies, and they believed drilling and exercising to be the basis for sound military training. In language typical of this period in both Australia and Britain, the Victorian Minister of Public Instruction voiced his support for drilling and exercising, commenting that 'apart from the physical pleasure and healthful character of military exercises, the lads should develop the smartness, the quickened attention, and the prompt obedience which military discipline begets'.[6] Indeed, there were many British boys who, according to Smith, had a good deal of fun playing soldier, particularly in performing manoeuvres that involved mock fighting and a chance to escape the confines of the classroom.[7] But there was also the more common experience of tedium, repetition and boredom associated with squad drill and adapted gymnastics exercises that, as we will see in Chapter 4, may have been more likely to develop sullen or grudging compliance rather than 'prompt obedience'.

In their earnest enthusiasm for making the new system of state-funded compulsory schooling work, this may have been too fine and subtle a distinction to warrant the attention of many colonial education bureaucrats who, like their political masters, also saw great value in drilling and exercising. The idea of attending school on a regular daily basis was new in the 1880s, and there was no tradition among the majority of the population of submitting willingly to hours of immobility at a school desk. In the British context, Smith reported that 'for those children in the first generation in the schools who attended against their own (and their parents') wishes . . . [their] . . . cooperation had to be enforced'.[8]

Economic factors were also influential in forming educational policy, and the proponents of 'national efficiency' in the early years of the new century, including the first Victorian Director of Education Frank Tate, drew drilling and exercising into the process of producing economically

31

productive citizens. Military drill and physical exercises seemed to offer a means of satisfying each of these needs for order and productivity. We might also note that drilling the body was entirely consistent with other school practices that adopted similar methods, such as the mechanistic recitation of times tables and the memorization of spelling and grammar.[9] So schools, their teachers and above all education authorities were understandably preoccupied with the question of how to gain compliance from potentially truculent pupils, so that maximum benefit could be extracted from the investment of public money. Drilling and exercising seemed to offer a useful solution to both problems.

Physical exercise in the first government controlled elementary schools of Australia and Britain thus came to be closely associated with military training. The development of militarist physical training in Britain during the last few decades of the nineteenth century has been described in some detail by Macintosh, Smith and Thomson, while the influence of these British developments on early physical training in New South Wales and Victoria has been examined exhaustively by Crawford.[10] In Australia, the colony of Victoria provides an illustrative example of the development of militarist drilling and exercising as a technology of power and the intention through these practices to drill bodies.

Militarism in the Ascendancy: The Case of Victoria

Physical training lessons were rare and sporadic in Victoria's early elementary schools, at least until the 1880s. One difficulty was a lack of qualified instructors to teach these lessons. In 1865, the Victorian Board of Education authorized Gustav Techow, Instructor at the National Gymnasium in Melbourne, to train elementary school teachers in military drill and gymnastics.[11] This initiative seems to have had mixed success. Enrolment in the course did not guarantee a pass, and the rewards were not high for teachers who were successful. Additional payments of fifteen pounds per annum were made to schools for the provision of military drill, but only half this amount for the teaching of gymnastics. Though Techow had been an officer in the Prussian army before arriving in Australia, he was first and foremost a gymnast and disciple of the Swede Per Henrick Ling, and drew a clear distinction between physical education and military work. So did the Victorian colonial government, but in contrast to Techow, it was military drill they valued most and, accordingly, it was military exercises they favoured in Victorian elementary schools.

The division of physical training into drill and gymnastics provides some evidence of the groups who had a stake in regular physical activity being provided in government schools. Gustav Techow was an early representative of a small but growing group of professional physical educators who had been trained in the Ling system of gymnastics, and who advocated gymnastics and games as broadly educational, rather than narrowly instrumental, activities. Techow's *Manual of Gymnastic Exercises*, published in 1866 primarily as a handbook for teachers undertaking his courses at the National Gymnasium, is a good example of the professional discourse and field of knowledge this group of physical educators in Australia, Europe, Britain and the USA were generating, accumulating and disseminating in the latter half of the nineteenth century.[12] For Techow, physical education in schools provided a counterbalance to intellectual pursuits. The equilibrium gained from regular participation in rational exercising was the wellspring of individual and, significantly, national achievement.

Techow harboured ambitions that the training scheme for teachers initiated by the Victorian government would bring about the wide dissemination of authoritative knowledge and practice of rational exercising among the general population. As it happened, his hopes were never to be realized, at least, not in the manner he had envisaged. Although Techow's manual was available from 1866, the Victorian government elected in 1874 to provide *A Manual of Squad, Company and Running Drill* for use in its schools, which was a version of the British Army manual of field exercises adapted by Colonel Anderson, the Commandant of Defence Forces.[13] Robert Ramsay, the Minister of Public Instruction in 1876, clarified what seems to have been a confused situation regarding the meaning of the term 'drill' by clearly differentiating between class drill which licensed teachers were considered proficient to teach and which all children experienced, and military drill which required specialist certification and was restricted to boys aged twelve to fourteen.[14]

This delineation of class and military drill was a form of compromise on the part of the Victorian government, intended to appease the more strident calls for schools to be utilized 'as the nurseries of the civil militia'[15] by making proficiency to teach at least class drill a condition of employment of licensed teachers. By 1884, in the face of further agitation for more military drill in schools and following New South Wales' example, the Victorian government introduced a voluntary military cadet scheme in schools for boys. In the furore surrounding this agitation, Techow's calls for a state-wide system of physical education based on gymnastics, which had little apparent military benefit, was less obviously effective as a means of instilling discipline, and which required the provision of expensive facilities, stood little chance of being heard.

Given the relatively favourable circumstances of increased payments to teachers and political support from the government, the numbers of schools in Victoria offering military drill grew steadily throughout the 1870s to the 1890s. In 1878, 111 schools offered military drill to 7457 boys. By 1888, the last year these classes came under the auspices of the Minister of Public Instruction and his Inspectors, this number had risen to 212 schools with 12,550 boys attending classes. During 1889, responsibility for the training of most elementary school teachers in military drill and for the inspection of military drill and physical training in schools was handed over to the Defence Department, on the basis of the view, vigorously argued by the military, that teachers required regular updating in physical training, which in turn required specialist staff. By 1893, the numbers of schools offering military drill had increased to 245, involving 18,700 boys and 358 trained teachers.[16]

In contrast, while gymnastics also grew over this period, the numbers of school pupils and teachers involved was markedly less due to the substantially higher payment to schools for running military drill classes. Compounding this factor, a frequent complaint made by School Inspectors was a lack of appropriate equipment and facilities. In 1882, only four schools in Victoria were offering gymnastics compared to 195 offering military drill; by 1893, this number had increased to seventeen schools against the 245 involved in military drill.[17] The recession of the 1890s certainly affected the operations of the Defence Department Inspectors, and retrenchments during 1893 resulted in less detailed coverage and reporting of activities in schools up to the turn of the century. The establishment of swimming clubs in state schools by the mid-1890s, which was one of the forces behind the formation of the Victorian State Schools Athletics Association in 1904,[18] offered the possibility for some children of participation in physical activities beyond military drill and physical exercises. Yet, despite the recession, retrenchments and the voluntary organization of extra-curricular sports by elementary school teachers, physical training in Victorian government schools was firmly embedded in militarism.

The military made no secret of their interest in the use of schools as a training ground for Australia's citizen army. The Australian colonies had been nervous about defence following the withdrawal of the last of the British forces in 1870, these anxieties fuelled by a perception that Russia and Japan had territorial ambitions which might include parts of the Australian continent. Consequently, sections of the military were keen to have a cadet scheme made compulsory for all boys aged twelve to eighteen. The Defence Department's Inspectors were also keen to argue that their specialized subject was different from other aspects of the school curriculum and required teachers to update their knowledge on the latest developments in military matters. But there were other motivations, beyond the transmission of the technicalities of marching, drilling and shooting a rifle. Reporting in 1889 after one year in the job as Inspectors of Physical Training in Victorian schools, Lieutenant Colonel Snee and Captain Henry remarked that 'the effect (of drill) on the general behaviour of the boys is becoming very marked, and with a compulsory system of drill, incipient larrikinism would receive a severe check, and the military spirit of the colony would be greatly fostered'.[19]

Among the Education Department's own staff, similar sentiments were regularly expressed. Inspector Charles Tynan of Melbourne's Metropolitan South District regarded class and military drill as a 'most valuable aid to discipline'[20] while, as we saw earlier in this chapter, the Minister himself believed that drill would instil in boys instant obedience to command. Others, less sanguine, recognized that the real benefits of drill were not so easily achieved. Inspector Ross Cox, writing in 1881, pointed out that 'in a few schools some of the movements of military drill are well gone through, but I have seen good wheeling and forming fours on the march, and other movements of the same kind, in schools where the really useful part of drill – the carriage and bearing of the boys – has been quite neglected. If time spent in teaching the movements was devoted to drilling boys into a soldierly way of carrying themselves, it would do them much more good than they receive at present.'[21]

The real value of both class and military drill, as Inspector Cox suggests, was in the fundamental effects it had on movement, carriage and deportment, and in the expectation that there would be a carryover to other aspects of children's conduct in school. None of this is to suggest that drill was an imposition on the girls and boys who experienced it, at least where it was well organized by enthusiastic staff.[22] But it was quite explicitly concerned with the shaping of pupils' bodies and movements, and the training and installation of a particular repertoire of behaviours, sentiments and responses. The extent to which these effects were achieved in schools is, of course, likely to have been variable. But there can be little question that the practice of drill had some cumulative effects both in terms of shaping children's bodies, and on the notion of schooling itself.

According to Gustav Techow and other professional gymnasts, there were clear differences of purpose and effect between drill and gymnastics. However, to the untutored observer of their practice, these distinctions would have seemed very fine indeed. Crawford[23] has described in some detail Techow's long and frustrating communications with the Victorian government between 1872 and 1884, in which he displayed a strong opposition to military and class drill, proposing instead a vision of physical education which promoted educational and health-related outcomes. But while this opposition to military training marks an important distinction, Techow's version of Lingian gymnastics, like many of the rival systems of the day, was deeply embedded in a discourse of discipline and regulation which had close affinities with the technology of power represented in drill.

The National Gymnasium, his base of operation, was established in 1864 by the Victorian government under the supervision of the

Colonel-Commandant of Volunteers. While Techow was careful in his 1866 manual to delineate 'purely military exercises' from educational activities, the pedagogy and some of the exercises and activities closely resembled each other. Teachers were to pronounce the words of command in a military fashion. The gymnastics class was to be arranged in military-style formation, and Techow outlined intricate details of spacing, alignment, distances, subdivisions and files. He also provided minute prescriptive details of bodily movements which differed not at all from the kind of detail found in military manuals.

Moreover, Techow suggested, 'discipline is almost as indispensable for a gymnasium as for an army'.[24] Each of the exercises in the manual were prescribed with the same exactitude, and were organized into tables which grouped, classified and sequenced them precisely. The tables were to be worked through in a set sequence according to the commands of the instructor, which were scripted alongside the exercises. When Techow referred to rational gymnastics as a 'systematic culture of the muscles', he was speaking literally. The overarching purpose was to gain control of the body in the most precise and intricate fashion, down to the level of individual groups of muscles, and to order and organize exactly bodies and their relation to each other in space.

Physical Training and Compulsory Military Training in Schools

As a result of these militaristic influences and developments, by the turn of the century in Australia physical training in the elementary schools of most states consisted mainly of military drill (marching, squad drill, rifle shooting) for boys aged 12 to 14, class drill for all boys and girls which was made up of the rudiments of military drill (such as marching and filing) and a few flexion and extension exercises drawn from the various systems of gymnastics available.[25] To this point the situation matched developments in Britain where the English Board of Education's *Model Course of Physical Training*, published in 1902, was based entirely on military drilling and exercising. However, there were already signs in Britain that the rise of militarism was about to be challenged. As Thomson[26] noted, there was widespread opposition to the Model Course from teachers, Lingian gymnasts and social reformers who claimed that many of the movements were anatomically unsound and actually harmful to growing children. In response, the author of the Model Course claimed that the social reformers were grossly exaggerating the physical condition of children in schools and that for many 'weakly' children, this form of physical training was highly desirable.[27]

In contrast to events in Britain, compulsory military training in schools continued to gain support in Australia following federation. Early versions of the voluntary cadet scheme in Victoria, which as we have seen had existed since 1885, along with similar schemes in Queensland and New South Wales with drilling and exercising at their core, were used as precedents in proposals circulating just after federation advocating control by the Commonwealth Defence Department of a compulsory military training scheme, which was to include boys at school. These proposals were entirely consistent with one of the major objectives of federation which was the establishment of a more efficient defence force than could be provided by the individual colonies.[28]

The legislative machinery to make this possible was provided by the 1903 Defence Act, including regulations and standing orders which enabled the Governor-General to establish and maintain a compulsory cadets scheme at both junior and senior levels. The main protagonist for compulsory military training in the first years of federation was William Morris Hughes, a Labour politician and later Prime Minister, who believed that a strong defence force developed through compulsory military training was the only sure means of enacting the White Australia policy enshrined in the Immigration Restriction Bill of 1901.[29]

The Victorian Minister of Public Instruction, A.O. Sachse, agreed with Hughes that this was the best way of providing for Australia's future defence needs, 'so that, from primary school, the nucleus of a true citizen soldiery for the purpose of national defence will be created'.[30] Sachse also expressed impatience with the Defence Department for what he perceived to be their tardiness in using the Act to set up the cadet training scheme. But there was considerable resistance to a scheme of compulsory military training in schools on the part of the various state Education Departments, and Sachse's political agenda did not necessarily match that of the public servants who staffed his department. By 1905, these education bureaucrats and teachers had been persuaded to attend a conference in Sydney at which they acceded to the Commonwealth Department of Defence's request to supervise the administration of the voluntary cadet scheme in their schools, on the condition that they 'interfere as little as possible and . . . leave the general control of the (cadet) movement to the Directors of Education and the executive details to the officers commanding'.[31] A major concern of the Directors of Education was that army personnel could have control over aspects of work in the schools and act without their authority.

There was also disagreement about who might finance a compulsory scheme, a matter which was to be an enduring issue. While not necessarily opposing the principle behind a compulsory junior cadet scheme, the Directors' fears that the Defence Department might assume a dictatorial role within schools were scarcely concealed. In December 1906, all states protested immediately and angrily when the Defence Department presumed to order officers away from their educational duties for a meeting to revise regulations without first consulting their respective Director of Education. In July 1907, the Prime Minister was forced to send a conciliatory letter to the Premier of South Australia reassuring him that the appointment of officers commanding cadets in any state 'will not be recommended without first seeking nomination from the Education Department'.[32]

Needless to say, these arrangements did not completely satisfy the Defence Department. They instructed the new state commandants to do all they could to increase the numbers of voluntary cadets in schools until such time as the scheme became compulsory. In Victoria, this task became the responsibility of Walter Gamble. A new voluntary Commonwealth-supervised military cadet scheme provided schoolboys with the incentive of a uniform and teachers and school inspectors were allowed commissions and military rank with improved promotion prospects in the school system. As a result, Gamble managed in a twelve-month period to double recruitment to junior cadets, which had been in rapid decline in Victoria between the 1890s and 1907.[33] Nevertheless, the Defence Department seemed determined that nothing less than a compulsory scheme would fulfil its aspirations. Early in 1907, the Acting Secretary to the Department of Defence wrote to inform the states that 'the Minister . . . in view of the vast importance of this subject to the Commonwealth is of the opinion that these revised regulations do not provide for sufficient increase of the cadet forces and submits for consideration the attached alternative schemes'.[34]

A compulsory scheme of cadet training was inaugurated in Queensland by 1906,[35] but while this precedent supported their case, the Department of Defence recognized that any attempts to involve schools in a scheme of purely military training were unlikely to succeed, despite the growing political support for such a scheme energetically engineered by Hughes, who made the most of public paranoia regarding the expansionist policies of some of Australia's Asian neighbours, the so-called Yellow Peril.[36] Instead, they decided to link their case for compulsory military training to a broader system of physical training which would be of benefit to all students.

However, it took a further two years and a letter from Prime Minister Andrew Fisher to convince the Education Departments to come to the conference table. In May 1909, prior to the establishment of the Defence Act of that year, Fisher wrote to the state premiers inviting them to nominate a delegate to attend a conference on physical training relating to a cadet training scheme. He went to some lengths to stress that a universal scheme of physical training was 'considered by the Defence department to form the basis on which any subsequent military training must depend'.[37] At the time, Fisher's Minister of State for Defence, Joseph Cook, had it in mind that 'a uniform system should be adopted throughout the Commonwealth'. While the Defence Act of 1909 provided the means of officially and formally conjoining compulsory military training and physical training for another twenty years, two conferences held in Melbourne in 1909 and 1910 played a crucial role in determining the kind of physical training that would form the basis of cadet training.

The Melbourne Conferences on Physical Training

The 1909 Conference was held, somewhat appropriately, at the Victoria Barracks in St. Kilda Road, Melbourne on 16–18 June and opened by Joseph Cook. Each state was represented, barring Queensland and Tasmania, and the Commonwealth Government delegate was the Surgeon-General Williams. Both Cook and Commander S.A. Pethebridge, Secretary to the Defence Department, withdrew after the official opening and, with Williams presiding, left the working party to get on with the job. The most intractable problem in the way of the Defence Department's plans was that the existing cadet schemes were effectively under the control of the state Education Departments, not the federal government. As one newspaper report rather perceptively expressed it, 'there cannot be two defence systems, one administered by the Education Departments up to 18 years of age, and thence forward by the Commonwealth'. At the same time, each side had interests to protect: 'the states will not give up the valuable training the boys get in their schools, and the Defence department cannot proceed to organise independent cadet battalions'.[38]

In the event, the delegates set about resolving this problem in a way that was designed to reconcile the conflicting interests of the two main parties. Their strategy was to avoid consideration of the matter of military training altogether, which was 'to be dealt with at a later stage by military officers',[39] and focus instead on the question of a 'uniform system of physical training of school boys in its relation to the physical fitness required for service as cadets which . . . should not be confined to cadets but extended to all children attending schools in the Commonwealth'.[40] Reflecting this tactic, the Conference's recommendations dealt solely with the appointment of staff to train instructors of cadets and teachers, the need for a central training facility, and the establishment of a system of physical training in the school curriculum and an accompanying manual.

This commitment to provide a scheme of physical training for the entire school population, on a national basis, and all at the expense of the Defence Department, was an offer the Education Departments could not refuse. The delegates' recommendations concerning the training of teachers by Defence Department instructors proved to be a key factor in securing a settlement.

The military physical training staff's role would be to train school teachers to run the scheme in the schools. There would therefore be no need for the military actually to enter the schools. Since the teachers were under the direct control of the Education Departments, this resolution was intended to remove the long-standing fears of the states that there would be an influx of independent army personnel into the schools.

Their fears were well founded, since they had the example from Britain of what could happen in just such a case. In order to implement the Model Course of 1902, a large number of former army NCO drill instructors had been appointed to schools. Generally poorly educated and completely ill-equipped to work with children, their presence in the schools was deeply resented by teachers and, according to Peter Macintosh,[41] had detrimental consequences for physical training that persisted long after the last of the NCOs left the teaching service in the early 1920s.

In a similar fashion to the Royal Commission on Physical Training in Scotland,[42] the Conference received submissions from a range of physical culturists on the perceived merits of the various systems of physical training that might form the basis of the new scheme. Surprisingly, given their professional and business interests in physical culture as private owners of gymnasia, Clarence Weber and H.C. Bjelke-Petersen gave strong support to a manual of military training produced in 1908, suggesting that with some adaptations this would be a suitable course of instruction for all children.[43] The Conference reserved judgement on the issue, however, recommending that the choice of a system and manual be left to the to-be-appointed Director of Physical Training, with the qualification that he submit the scheme to the Defence Authorities and the state Education Departments for approval prior to implementation.

Of the five men in attendance at the Conference, at least three had already demonstrated strong support for a compulsory national cadet scheme in schools. Surgeon-General Williams at the time was the Director-General of Medical Services and Cadets; Colonel R.E. Roth, while an advocate of the Swedish system of gymnastics, also believed that 'every boy should be compelled to serve in the cadets';[44] and the Victorian Director of Education Frank Tate, with his commitment to individual and national efficiency, had sympathies for a uniform scheme of physical training in schools.[45] The agreements reached by these five men set the agenda for what was to follow and in the process cut through a range of contentious issues surrounding the notion of a compulsory scheme of military training which were to surface later.

At no time during the Conference of 1909 or at the subsequent Conference of 1910 were any doubts expressed in the official record concerning the essentially military purposes which underpinned the scheme.[46] The delegates reached agreement after only two days of discussion of a matter that had stalled the Commonwealth and the states for the previous seven years suggesting, perhaps, that the parties now believed they had found a key to achieving a settlement which suited both.

Twelve men representing a broader set of interests attended a second Conference on Physical Training held in Melbourne in March 1910. Ostensibly, this second Conference was convened to amend the recommendations of the previous year's Conference in light of changes to the Defence Act of 1909. This Act proposed a defence scheme involving compulsory military training for youths up to 26 years of age. At William Hughes' invitation, Lord Kitchener had visited Australia in December 1909, and through to February 1910 inspected existing military training arrangements. The scheme was based on his advice and was incorporated into the Defence Act.[47] Consequently, the second Conference was forced to consider only those matters of relevance to the training of boys covered by the Act, on the face of it undoing the 1909 Conference's recommendation for a scheme of physical training to cover all school children.

While this was indeed the formal position, the delegates inserted the qualification that, in their collective opinion, 'the State Education Departments and the proprietors and head masters of schools not under the State Departments be urged to provide in the curriculum of their schools a system of physical training for all school boys and girls respectively'.[48] The formal Conference recommendations reinforced this point by making provision for the training of teachers by the Defence Force instructors at the federal government's expense, which had been a key to the settlement achieved in the earlier Conference. The promise of the first Conference to provide a system of physical training appropriate to the entire school population was also to be honoured by the second Conference's recommendation that the 1909 British Syllabus of Physical Exercises[49] be used to form the basis of physical training in all government schools.

The second Melbourne Conference included four of the previous year's delegates (only Roth was missing) along with representatives of the school registration boards, teachers' associations, private schools and the medical profession. Queensland and Tasmania again did not send delegates. There was a clear concern for a scientific approach to physical training with an emphasis on improving health, perhaps due to the presence of Dr Harvey Sutton and Alex Leeper. Leeper, representing the private schools, was particularly wary of the damage that could be done to children by an unskilled teacher and believed there was 'considerable quackery in the ranks of the physical culturists'.[50] The Conference recommended that a thoroughly qualified 'expert' who possessed a 'knowledge of anatomy, physiology and of the physiology of physical exercise' should be appointed Commonwealth Director of Physical Training. Similar knowledge was expected to form an essential part of cadet training. The Conference also recommended, clearly on the advice of Sutton, that the medical inspection of school children, which had just begun in Victoria under his direction, be coordinated to complement the new system of physical training and ensure that medically unfit children were not forced to exert themselves.[51]

These factors suggest the delegates were aware of some of the possible dangers of a scheme of school physical training shaped solely by military interests, and suggest too some softening of the ideas of the previous decade that children's bodies needed to be drilled in a regimented fashion to instil prompt obedience. It is also possible that some delegates at the Conference were aware of the push for compulsory military training in Britain some eight years earlier and the outcome of these events.

In 1898, a strong militarist lobby led by Sir Henry Craik, Secretary of the Scottish Education Department, attempted to promote the practice of systematic military training in schools following the unexpected defeats of British troops at the hands of the Boers.[52] But the militarists' plans met stiff resistance from the local School Boards and the teaching profession. In March 1902 Lord Balfour, Secretary of State for Scotland, and initially sympathetic to the militarists' cause, requested permission from Cabinet to appoint a Royal Commission on Physical Training to review provision for physical training in Scottish elementary schools. The Commission was appointed later that year and subsequently reported in 1903. Although the initial line of inquiry tended towards consideration of the merits of military drill, the Commissioners were impressed by Inspectors', School Boards' and teachers' reasoned resistance to military training. They were also impressed by submissions based on surveys of the health of school children, and their consideration of this evidence resulted in an important shift in emphasis between their initial remit and their Report.

The Commission's key recommendations, which we will consider in more detail in the next chapter, were that the British Government introduce regular medical inspections of pupils and schools meals. They also recommended the establishment of a committee to devise a syllabus of physical exercises for schools, which appeared in 1904, in a revised edition in 1905 and again in 1909, the third syllabus showing for the first time a clear preference for the Ling system of Swedish gymnastics set within a therapeutic framework. In effect, these recommendations ended the militarist push for compulsory military training and physical training in British elementary schools which was firmly located within a medical rationale administered by the School Medical Service following its establishment in 1908. While obedience and discipline remained a requirement, the 1909 syllabus, which was to form the basis of the new syllabus for Australian schools, encouraged a less regimented approach by teachers and introduced some less formal activities such as dancing. At the same time, we might note that these changes were to be implemented by ill-trained teachers and the ex-army drill instructors who would, without doubt, have made a militarist interpretation of the syllabus.

The British experience would certainly have been well known to Sutton, who was completing a research degree at Oxford between 1905–8,[53] and to other delegates such as Leeper and L.A. Adamson, the headmaster of Wesley College and a staunch Anglophile. Adamson was a strong supporter of cadet training, but also believed firmly in the merits of the English games tradition.[54] Sutton had competed for Australia in the 880 yards at the London Olympics and was also an advocate of games and sport in schools. Between them, Adamson and Sutton were instrumental in the Conference recording its desire to stress 'the importance of swimming and organised games in all schools where such may be practical'.[55]

The System of Physical Training

The Ling system of gymnastics was used by various armies and navies as the basis of their physical fitness programmes, though it was designed by Ling and his predecessors as a system of therapeutic exercises, a factor that won the support of school medical services in Australia and Britain.[56] The free-standing exercises were popular with institutions because they could be performed by large groups requiring little space, and were based on systematic exercise progressions that proponents claimed provided a general foundation for all-round, symmetrical physical development. The physical fitness, health and skill benefits provided an appropriately benevolent justification for the system, but Swedish gymnastics was attractive to education authorities because it also came with a formal pedagogy which required uniform activity from pupils and instant response to command.

Given some of the Melbourne Conference delegates' doubts about overtly militaristic systems of physical training, the Conference's strong recommendation of the British 1909 Syllabus of Physical Exercises as the basis of the physical training system left little to chance, since this decision over-turned the recommendation of the previous Conference that the choice of syllabus should be in the hands of the Defence Department's Director of Physical Training. As it turned out, Hans-Christian Bjelke-Petersen was appointed Director of Physical Training in 1912, and he had suggested to the 1909 Conference that a 1908 military manual would be an adequate basis for the system of physical training. The 1910 Conference's recommendation was enacted, though not until 1916 when the Junior Cadet Training Manual eventually appeared. It consisted of the entire British syllabus with several additional sections on military training, anatomy and physiology.[57]

In the physical training sections, lessons were scripted in the form of tables that dealt, in a systematic fashion, with the major joints and muscle groups of the body. The tables themselves were organized in an immutable sequence according to the age and experience of the pupils (see Table 2.1). This was, in other words, an entire physical training program, with the progressions, sequencing and age standards mapped out in detail.

Table 2.1 Programme of work in physical training, *Junior Cadet Training Manual*, 1916

Series	Approximate Age of the Pupils	Years of Work in Physical Exercises	First	Terms Second	Third
A	7–8	First	1–4	5–8	9–12
	8–9	Second	13–16	17–20	21–24
B	9–10	Third	25–28	29–32	33–36
	10–11	Fourth	37–40	41–44	45–48
C	11–12	Fifth	49–52	53–56	57–60
	12–14	Sixth	61–64	65–68	69–72

The actual lessons themselves were set out in a format that also had to be adhered to strictly. There were eight categories of activities, and each lesson was constructed on the basis of a selection of exercises from each category. The categories were, in order of appearance in the lesson:

1 Introduction and breathing exercises.
2 Trunk bending back and forward.
3 Arm bending and stretching.
4 Balance exercises.
5 Shoulder-blade exercises (Abdominal exercises).
6 Trunk turning and bending sideways.
7 Marching, running, jumping, games, etc.
8 Breathing exercises.

Teachers were required to memorize the precise series of exercises for each lesson, and to deliver their instructions using such commands as 'head backwards – bend!', 'left foot sideways – place!', 'trunk forward and downward – stretch!' and 'knees – bend!' These commands were amended to 'suit Australian conditions' in 1922 and again in 1926, but the militaristic flavour persisted.

For instance, lesson 2 in the sequence outlined in the 1922 edition of the *Junior Cadet Training Textbook*[58] begins in the following fashion:

1. Free running in large circle. Instant halt on signal.
   Double – march! Class – halt!
   Run to form one rank at wall; place leaders on marks; run to open ranks.
   Back to the wall – move! Leaders on markers – move! To your places – move!
2. (Astride) Trunk bending downward to grasp ankles.
   (With a jump, feet astride – place!) Grasping both ankles – down! Class – up! and etc. (with a jump, feet together – place!).

This new scheme of junior cadet training coupled with the Ling system of gymnastics became a reality in March 1911. Approval was given for training that 'must occupy not less than fifteen minutes each day, and will consist of elementary drill, miniature rifle shooting, swimming, running . . . exercise(s) in organised games, and first aid' and for the boys to 'be trained by authorised schoolmasters, or by members of the administrative and instructional staff'.[59] Physical exercises and military drill formed the mandatory aspects of the scheme, and schools could elect to offer two from the range of other activities listed, including mariner's compass training and elementary signalling.

Drilled Bodies

The structure of the 1916 Australian Junior Cadet Training text and its 1909 British prototype, while considered by teachers to be an improvement on those army manuals that had preceded them, continued to embody a technology of biopower that had been used to drill the bodies of previous generations of working-class children. In Britain, the persistent presence of the ex-army drill instructors until after the First World War meant that the softer tone of the 1909 syllabus would hardly have been noticed by the pupils themselves, while in the Australian states, the Ling system was firmly attached to a scheme of military training for older boys. Moreover, the male teachers of these junior cadets and of the girls and younger boys were trained by army physical training instructors, as were the female instructors of female teachers.

There can be no question that the intention behind these syllabuses remained that of regulating children's behaviour through detailed and intricate work on their bodies. Lieutenant-Colonel Bjelke-Petersen, the first Director of Physical Training, was adamant that standards should not be compromised when the matter of training instructresses for the scheme was raised in 1913, arguing that 'it is so essential that all details be taught correctly, as the secret of success in the Dano-Swedish System of Physical

Training is absolute correct performance of each exercise in order to accomplish the object for which it was designed. It has been my experience "that to teach a subject quickly means inferior work".[60] Bjelke-Petersen well knew that in performing these exercises with absolute correctness and precision children and their teachers were at the same time being trained to move only in certain ways and not others. Herein lay the strength of militarized physical training as a technology of power, and also its great weakness; for unless the prescriptions for movement were performed exactly, their regulative effects were severely reduced. Meticulous attention to detail was everything, and as we will see in Chapter 4, without it this form of schooling bodies was more likely to produce the opposite effects from those intended, to construct resisting rather than drilled bodies.

While militarist practices continued their ascendancy in Australia, two developments were to slow their progress. The first of these was the First World War and its aftermath, a matter we turn to in Chapter 4. A second development was the growing influence of a public health lobby and the discourse of eugenics, that shared militarist physical training's concern to work in meticulous detail on the body, but that also stressed the therapeutic values inherent in forms of physical activity that might combat physical deterioration rather than exacerbate it, and act as a means of preventing poor health. It is to the emergence of school medical inspection and anthropometry that we now turn in Chapter 3.

Notes and References

1 Smith, W.D. (1974) *Stretching Their Bodies: The History of Physical Education* London: David & Charles, p. 92.
2 Francis, R.I. (1979) Schools from the pupils' point of view: New South Wales in the late colonial period *Journal of the Australian and New Zealand History of Education Society*, **8** (2), 2, pp. 22–35.
3 Thomson, I. (1979) Over-pressure and physical deterioration factors leading to the acceptance of physical education 1880–1895 *Physical Education Review*, **2** (2), pp. 115–22.
4 Smith, *Stretching Their Bodies*.
5 See e.g. the Australasian Association for the Advancement of Science *AAAS Conference Proceedings*, 1902/3.
6 Minister of Public Instruction (1885) *Education Report for the Year 1884–85* Melbourne: Government Printer, p. xxiii.
7 Smith, *Stretching Their Bodies*, p. 91.
8 Smith, *Stretching Their Bodies*, p. 94.
9 Francis, Schools from the pupils' point of view.
10 Macintosh, P.C. (1968) *Physical Education in England Since 1800* London: Bell (2nd edn); Smith, *Stretching Their Bodies*; Thompson, I. (1978) The origins of

Physical Education in State Schools *Scottish Educational Review*, **10** (2),
pp. 17–34; Crawford, R. (1981) A history of physical education in Victoria and
New South Wales 1872–1939: with particular reference to English precedent.
Unpublished PhD Thesis, La Trobe University.

11 Minister of Public Instruction (1865) *Education Report for the Year 1864–65*
Melbourne: Government Printer; Techow, G. (1866) *Manual of Gymnastic
Exercises for the Use of Schools and at Home* Melbourne: George Robertson.

12 See the comparative sections of Smith, *Stretching Their Bodies*, pp. 102–5, 128–31
for a useful overview of these developments.

13 Department of Education, Victoria (1874) *A Manual of Squad, Company and
Running Drill* Melbourne: Government Printer.

14 Minister of Public Instruction (1876) *Education Report for the Year 1875–76*
Melbourne: Government Printer.

15 Crawford, A history of physical education, p. 79.

16 Minister of Public Instruction (1879) *Education Report for the Year 1878–79*
Melbourne: Government Printer; Minister of Public Instruction (1889) *Education
Report for the Year 1888–89* Melbourne: Government Printer; Minister of Public
Instruction (1890) *Education Report for the Year 1889–90* Melbourne:
Government Printer; Minister of Public Instruction (1894) *Education Report for
the Year 1893–94* Melbourne: Government Printer.

17 Minister of Public Instruction (1883) *Education Report for the Year 1882–83*
Melbourne: Government Printer.

18 Education Department, Victoria (1904, July), *Education Gazette and Teachers' Aid*
Melbourne: Government Printer.

19 Minister of Public Instruction Report, 1890, p. 264.

20 Minister of Public Instruction (1881) *Education Report for the Year 1880–81*
Melbourne: Government Printer, p. 195.

21 Minister of Public Instruction Report, 1881, p. 205.

22 Minister of Public Instruction Report, 1881, p. 208.

23 Crawford, A history of physical education.

24 Techow, *Manual of Gymnastic Exercises*, p. 143.

25 Crawford, A history of physical education.

26 Thomson, The origins of Physical Education in State Schools, p. 21.

27 Smith, *Stretching Their Bodies*, p. 108.

28 Inglis, K.S. (1968) Conscription in peace and war, in Forward, R. and Reece, B.
(eds) *Conscription in Australia* St. Lucia, Brisbane: University of Queensland
Press, pp. 22–58

29 Booker, M. (1982) Billy Hughes and Australian defence *Hemisphere*, **26**,
January/February, pp. 211–13. Booker notes that by 1905 Hughes had managed to
enlist support for his ideas on military training from a range of wealthy and
influential members of the community. On Hughes' defence ambitions and the
White Australia policy, see Inglis, Conscription in peace and war, p. 24.

30 Minister of Public Instruction (1905) *Education Report for the Year 1904–5*
Melbourne: Government Printer, p. 16.

31 Australian Archives Victoria (AAV), MP 84/1 Department of Defence, 1832/13/40
and 1832/12/502.

32 AAV, MP 84/1, 1832/8/89, letter from the Prime Minister to the Premier of South
Australia, 24 August 1907.

33 Minister of Public Instruction (1907) *Education Report for the Year 1906–7* Melbourne: Government Printer, p. 19.

34 AAV, MP 84/1, 1832/8/20, letters from the Acting Secretary to the Department of Defence to the Under Secretary for Public Instruction in all States, 15 February 1907.

35 AAV, MP 84/1, 1832/13/90, letters from the Queensland Government to the Prime Minister, 1910–11.

36 Fears of the so-called Yellow Peril were inspired by Japan's defeat of Russia at Mukden in 1905 and by Australian racism, see Inglis, Conscription in peace and war, p. 25.

37 AAV, MP 84/1, 1832/1/220, letter to the State Premiers from Prime Minister Fisher, 10 May 1909.

38 *Argus*, 21 June 1909, p. 4.

39 *Argus*, 19 June 1909.

40 AAV, MP 84/1, 1832/1/220, Report of the 1909 Melbourne Conference on Physical Training.

41 Macintosh, *Physical Education in England*, p. 149.

42 Board of Education/Scottish Education Department (1903) *Royal Commission on Physical Training (Scotland)* London: HMSO.

43 Clarence Weber, see the *Australian Dictionary of Biography*, 7, 1891–1939, p. 430; Hans Christian Bjelke-Petersen was later to be appointed Commonwealth Director of Physical Training with the honorary rank of Lieutenant-Colonel, a position he held from 1911–14. In 1918–20 he was an inspector of physical training for the Department of Defence and an honorary consultant to the military forces between 1920–22, see the *Australian Dictionary of Biography*, 7, 1891–1939, p. 300.

44 Roth, R.E. (1904) *Australian Journal of Education*, 2 (2) pp. 7–8.

45 Frank Tate, see the *Australian Dictionary of Biography*, 12, 1891–1939, pp. 169–72; and Crawford, A History of Physical Education, p. 250.

46 The apparent ambivalence among the general community before 1910 to militarism, the question of compulsory training and the passage of the 1909 Defence Act has been noted by several writers. They suggest, variously, that the Defence Act was enacted during a great coal strike, preoccupying public attention, see Jauncey, L.C. (1935) *The Story of Conscription in Australia* London: Allen & Unwin, p. 35; that the adult community was largely unaffected personally, according to Hurley, F.T. (1972) Compulsory military training and the conscription referendum 1911–1916. Unpublished MA thesis, University of Melbourne, p. 50; or that it was unclear, according to Inglis, whether it was 'ignorance, apathy or hostility' at work in relation to non-registration of senior cadets in years subsequent to the establishment of the scheme, Inglis, Conscription in peace and war, p. 27.

47 Mordike, J.L. (1984) Lord Kitchener's memorandum on the defence of Australia, 1910 *Defence Force Journal*, 47, July/August, pp. 43–51.

48 AAV, MP 84/1, 1832/1/220, Report of the 1910 Melbourne Conference on Physical Training, p. 2.

49 Board of Education (1909) *Syllabus of Physical Exercises for Schools* London: HMSO.

50 *Argus*, 3 September 1911, p. 5.

51 AAV, MP 84/1, 1832/1/220, Report of the 1910 Melbourne Conference, p. 3.

52 Thompson, I. (1986) Militarism and Scottish schools in the Boer War era *Physical Education Review*, **8** (2), pp. 110–19.

53 Harvey Sutton, see the *Australian Dictionary of Biography*, **12**, 1891–1939, p. 143.

54 *Argus*, 12 August 1911; see also Crawford, R. (1986) Athleticism, gentleman and empire in Australian public schools: L.A. Adamson and Wesley College, Melbourne, in *Sport & Colonialism in 19th century Australasia* Sydney: ASSH, pp. 42–64.

55 AAV, MP 84/1, 1832/1/220, Report of the 1910 Melbourne Conference, p. 2.

56 Macintosh, *Physical Education in England*.

57 Australian Military Forces (1916) *Junior Cadet Training* Melbourne: Government Printer.

58 Department of Defence (1922) *Junior Cadet Training Textbook* Melbourne: Government Printer.

59 *Argus*, 4 March 1911, p. 18.

60 AAV, MP 84/1, 1832/13/573, 17 June 1912, internal minute paper to Adjutant General.

3

Examining Bodies: School Anthropometrics and Medical Inspection

> The examination combines the techniques of an observing hierarchy and those of a normalizing judgement. It is a normalizing gaze, a surveillance that makes it possible to qualify, to classify, and to punish. It establishes over individuals a visibility through which one differentiates them and judges them. That is why, in all the mechanisms of discipline, the examination is highly ritualized. In it are combined the ceremony of power and the form of the experiment, the deployment of force and the establishment of truth. At the heart of the procedures of discipline, it manifests the subjection of those who are perceived as objects and the objectification of those who are subjected. The superimposition of the power relations and knowledge relations assumes in the examination all its visible brilliance.[1]

Foucault suggested that the examination, as an institutionalized practice, is a means of individualization and differentiation. It is a practice intimately bound up with the work of schools, and it has played a central part in schooling bodies, both as a pedagogical tool and as a more specialized strategy of medical inspection. Once each individual was known, Foucault argued that she or he could be judged against a normative standard, and any behaviour that deviated from the norm could then be revealed in 'all its visible brilliance'. Through this technology of power, the examined body was a constitutive element of the schooled body. In medical inspection as it emerged and developed from the turn of the century, precision and detail were all important, since it was only through close attention to detail that appropriate differentiation between children could be made.

Concerns for the health of school children, and the view that medical inspection based on detailed examinations of children's bodies might help ameliorate poor health, were not confined to Australia. Indeed, both Australia and Britain were rather slow to respond at government level to the opportunities afforded by schools to intervene in the cause of improving public health. As early as the 1870s, western European countries such as Belgium and France had begun to appoint medical officers to their school systems. By the beginning of the First World War school medical inspection had been established in many European countries, in North America and in some Central and South American countries, and in Japan. The extent of the service offered, the duties and responsibilities given to medical officers, and the financial support made available for their work varied across and within countries. Despite these variations, much of this work was under-pinned by the conviction that preventative rather than curative medicine offered a better option to improved public health.[2]

The establishment of school medical inspection in Australia and Britain towards the end of the first decade of the twentieth century was based on the premise that the careful examination and measurement of children's bodies would lead to more efficient and productive generations of adults, workers and citizens. This premise found legitimacy in the explanations and solutions to questions of human propagation and breeding proffered by eugenicists, whose theories, as we saw in Chapter 1, had a powerful and widespread impact on many intellectuals and professionals in Europe, the United States of America and Australia.

The early years of the school medical services in Australia provide one avenue for exploration of shifts in the regulation of the individual body and the social body during the first half of this century. The strategies adopted by the Victorian school medical service in particular, linking medical inspection closely with anthropometric surveys, shows the intermeshing of regulatory and normative concerns. These strategies, developed between 1909 and 1915, illustrate the optimistic view that intimate and detailed quantitative know-ledge of children's bodies could provide a basis for medical and educational interventions which would significantly improve the physical, moral and social condition of the white race in Australia. While much of this work was in progress before 1902, the Report of the Royal Commission on Physical Training in Britain provided an important source of legitimacy for Australians interested in pursuing an agenda of public health reform that positioned schools as a key site of intervention. This chapter overviews developments in Britain and then explores their influence on the establishment of school anthropometry and medical inspection in Australia.

The Royal Commission on Physical Training and the Establishment of Medical Services in Britain

In Britain, social reformers advocated intervention through government schools as a major strategy for securing better public health, and while their underlying motivations varied, much effort was expended to secure better living conditions and better health for people who often lived in squalor, who were malnourished, who had physical and mental disabilities, and who had access to few resources that might enable them to fight against contagious disease. The Royal Commission on Physical Training was established 'to inquire into the opportunities for physical training now available in state-aided schools' in Scotland. However, the Commission's agenda was shaped substantially by other factors. It was sitting at a time when the rejection of large numbers of recruits for the British army's South African campaign was a newsworthy scandal that had stimulated widespread public interest and concern. This scandal served to highlight evidence that had been amassed by philanthropists and social reformers during the previous three decades of the appalling cases of malnutrition, dirt and disease among the poor.[3]

The report of the Commission was to provide a major stimulus to the establishment of medical services in England and Scotland through their respective Education Acts of 1907 and 1908. As was so often the case in such matters, this new determination by the British government to tackle the problem of public health lent support and legitimacy to the arguments of reformers who had been advocating the need for school medical inspection in Australia in the years leading up to the Commission. The Royal Commission on Physical Training was also important to Australian developments in physical training since the location of physical training within the school medical service in England led to the selection for schools of the therapeutically oriented Ling system of gymnastics. While as we saw in Chapter 2, Australian physical training was, ostensibly, embedded in a militarist framework, the Board of Education's 1909 Syllabus, based on the Ling system, formed the majority of the 1916 Australian Junior Cadet text.

In this context of apparent social and physical deterioration, the Commissioners' believed they could not comment on appropriate forms of physical training without first having some current information on the physical condition of children in Scottish schools, and so they commissioned a survey by Professor Matthew Hay and Dr W. Leslie McKenzie that compared the height, weight and general condition of health of children in Edinburgh and Aberdeen. This report of the physical examination of some 1200 children was accepted as a very valuable piece of evidence by the Commissioners and did much to persuade them of the necessity of a system of medical inspection in schools.

The Commissioners accepted too the idea that exercise could not cure disease, but properly conducted could have a beneficial effect on minor defects and deformities. The notion of 'nutrition' lay at the core of the Commission's views on health; it was 'the unifying concept which brought together the four component parts of a sound approach to improving health, namely food, clothing, fresh air and exercise'.[4] It was also accepted by the

Commissioners that the wrong kind of exercise, or exercise for under-nourished children, could have a deleterious effect. The main impact of the Commission's recommendations was to encourage the government of the day to empower the School Boards to introduce regular and systematic medical inspections and school meals.

The Royal Commission on Physical Training did not, by itself, create school medical inspection, and the reports of several other committees were required before the legislation was enacted in 1907. A school medical service within the Board of Education was formally established in 1908 with Dr (later Sir) George Newman as its Chief Medical Officer. While Newman was a strong advocate of physical training, overseeing the publication of three syllabuses between 1909 and 1933, the real work in maintaining the health of school children was from the beginning to be done through medicine. At first, the school medical service merely inspected children, but by 1912 grants were made available for treatment as well as inspection, and by the end of the First World War, inspections had been extended from elementary to all state-aided schools.[5] Consonant with these developments, student teachers in training were required to become familiar with 'the main principles of healthy living' and the maintenance of 'hygienic conditions in every part of school work'.

Writing in 1909, Hogarth summarized the many reasons advanced for public health interventions in schools during the previous decades, ranging from alleged physical deterioration of the race to underfeeding, and the prevention of contagion to the deleterious effects of attending school itself. He rejected all of these reasons and concluded that 'the interference of the State is essentially justified by the large amount of preventable and remediable defects among school children. These defects are unrecognised either by teachers or parents, and can only be discovered by systematic medical inspection.'[6] Whatever the truth of his claim, Hogarth's views on the necessity of 'systematic medical inspection' reflected a position adopted with considerable conviction of school medical officers in Australia.

School Anthropometry in Australia

Anthropometric testing linked to medical inspection was viewed by Australian eugenicists as one basis for preventative action. In his 1902 presidential address to the Australasian Association for the Advancement of Science, New South Wales government statistician T.A. Coghlan articulated some of these links explicitly.

As a first step towards (achievement of the ideal human type), it is necessary to determine a standard by which physical development may be tested. This can be done by taking measurements of a large number of children and summarising the results according to approved methods . . . . The scope of the anthropometrist working in Australia must therefore lie principally in noting the differences which develop themselves in people of the same race living under different social conditions; and I think Australian observations will tend to confirm the conclusions of observers elsewhere, that not to heredity, but to environment, must be attributed the major differences that are discernible among children of the same race who are born healthy.[7]

At the same meeting of the AAAS at which Coghlan delivered this speech, Hans-Christian Bjelke-Petersen, physical culturist and later to become the first Director of Physical Training for the Commonwealth Junior Cadet Training Scheme[8] presented the results of an anthropometric study of Hobart schoolboys. Bjelke-Petersen's objective was to obtain 'a more exact knowledge about the physical development of Tasmanian boys and the wish to compare them with other races'.[9] Bjelke-Petersen and an assistant examined over 500 boys, collecting data on the racial origins of the boys and a range of measures of their physical dimensions. On the basis of this information, he concluded that the rates of growth of Tasmanian boys was superior to that of comparable American and English boys, that compared with German and Belgian boys the Tasmanians were tallest for the first five years and were then overtaken by the Germans, that Sydney boys by Coghlan's measurements were considerably taller than Hobart boys and that when the average height of boys between the ages eight to fifteen from ten different countries and states were compared, New South Wales ranked second, and Tasmania eighth. Bjelke-Petersen concluded, on the basis of this and other American anthropometric data, that 'the bright pupil has fewest physical irregularities of growth, the dull pupils score slightly higher, while the criminal boys are leading by a long way. These lines indicate that the normal boy is likely to be the best boy morally.'[10]

On the basis of studies and advocacy such as these, anthropometry linked to medical inspection began to be seen by Australian eugenicists as a vital means of providing a baseline of detailed and precise information for government intervention through mass schooling. At the 1911 Conference of the AAAS, two formal resolutions were passed recommending that all anthropometric surveys carried out in Australia conform to standards established by their British counterparts and that the existing schemes of medical inspection and compulsory cadet training be utilized to permit a national survey to take place. These recommendations were supported in a presentation by Mary Booth, at the time one of the Victorian school medical officers, on the subject of school anthropometrics.[11] Booth considered anthropometry to be the 'physical basis of the enquiry as to whether heredity or environment is the more potent influence in his mental and physical development – that is the determination of the relation of man to his environment and to the laws of human evolution'. As part of her rationale for a national anthropometric survey of Australian schoolchildren, Booth claimed 'the eugenicist, in conformity with modern thought that science has its highest sanction when it is of service to man, makes use of the data of anthropometry for his study of what the race may become'. She argued that a properly conducted survey would enable Australians to 'recognise the modifications (if any) which the new environment or Anglo-Celtic mixture of our population is producing. The problem of settling the Northern Territory is particularly inviting to an anthropometric survey, and can only be adequately solved by demonstrating how far the white race can control an unfavourable environment.'

Booth cited a range of studies in Belgium, Germany, Britain and the United States, as well as the work of Coghlan in Sydney and Bjelke-Petersen in Hobart, as precedents for the kind of survey which might be carried out in Australia on a national basis, arguing for the importance of adopting uniform standards of measurement and method which might allow comparisons of Australian data with the findings of these other studies. The essential elements of a successful Australian survey for Booth included the careful selection of the kinds of data to be collected, uniform methods of collection according to the British Standard set in 1908 by the British Association for the Advancement of Science, and the statistical treatment of data. Only by including these elements could Australian studies 'have any scientific value or give results of practical use to the nation'.

Given the enormity of the task and its resource implications, Booth's strategy was to link the anthropometric survey to regular medical inspection of school children and junior cadets and to enlist the assistance of teachers on the condition that 'care is taken to instruct them in the need for accuracy, and to stimulate their interest by showing them a practical use for measurements of heights and weights as giving opportunities for problems in arithmetic and for graph work with their pupils'.[12] Following the conference, and on the basis of these resolutions and the rationale presented by Booth on behalf of the Anthropometric Committee, the Australian Association for the Advancement of Science requested in a letter to the Prime Minister that a national anthropometric survey of school pupils take place.

Others set about the task of urging the government to accept these proposals. At the same conference in 1911, another school medical officer and colleague of Booth, Harvey Sutton, presented some of the data collected by the school medical officers on the racial origins of Victorian children, arguing that such empirical data was the only rational basis for debating issues of Australian nationhood which had been achieving much popular attention at that time. Using a simple system of classification, he concluded that over 60 per cent of children in Victorian schools were Australian-born of Australian-born parents, suggesting that these children represented the 'first fruits of the Australian nation'.[13] Sutton argued that the White Australia policy was only practicable if the northern half of the continent could be populated successfully by Anglo-Celts. He suggested that a simpler means of reckoning the chances of successful settlement in these areas than sending proposed scientific expeditions to the Northern Territory would be to incorporate the system of classification he had outlined as part of a national anthropometric survey, which would identify 'at the earliest possible moment what influence the environment of southern land and skies is having on our race'.[14]

In the same year, Sutton presented his views on methods of classifying and dealing with the feeble-minded to the Australian Medical Conference. He described methods of mental testing adapted from the Binet-Simon system which he had applied to the detection and classification of 'idiots, imbeciles and feeble-minded' in conjunction with school medical inspection. Reporting the detection of some 317 cases of feeble-mindedness in 79 Melbourne schools, Sutton argued for the segregation and education of these children on humanitarian, social, economical and racial grounds. While the lot of those children judged to be feeble-minded by such mental testing was to be improved so far as possible through education and training, it is clear that Sutton approved of the control of their capacity to reproduce: 'one of the principles of eugenics is to eliminate in ideal fashion, stocks definitely undesirable . . . for if you do not help to check their increase, you and your children will have to pay for their support'.[15]

It seemed that all of the argumentation in support of a national anthropometric survey had borne fruit. However, the Anthropometric Committee and its allies' triumph was short-lived. Disaster struck as the survey was about to get under way. Just before their distribution to the states in 1913, the entire collection of cards and other information essential to the implementation of the survey were destroyed by fire while in the possession of the acting honorary secretary, Dr Bremand, who was almost immediately afterwards mobilized for war duty. No further action could be taken to repair the damage, and the activities of the Committee were immediately suspended, only recommencing in 1921.[16] While the intention was to resume where it had left off in 1913, the Committee appointed in 1921 did not meet during 1922. By 1923, though the Committee was again reappointed with a view to coordinating anthropometry throughout the Commonwealth, the impetus for a national survey had clearly been lost,[17] substantiating the claims of Bacchi, Cawte and Garton (see Chapter 1) that social reformers began to attend more closely to the solutions offered by negative eugenics.

School Medical Inspection

Before fire brought a premature end to the planned national anthropometric survey in 1913, school medical services had been prepared to play a key role in the collection of data and in the training of teachers to assist in this task. School medical services were instituted by most Australian state Education Departments in the 1910s. The British Medical Association (BMA) of Australia, which claimed the membership of the majority of Australian doctors, officially gave its approval, commenting that 'those who are concerned with the health of Nations recognise that the care of the infant and of the school child is the first factor in the building up of a strong race'.[18] In Victoria, the school medical service was established in November 1909 staffed by three medical officers, Dr Mary Booth, Dr Jane Greig and Dr Harvey Sutton. Greig was to remain with the service until she retired in 1936 as Chief Medical Inspector, while Sutton went on to a career as Professor of Tropical Medicine at the University of Sydney and Booth became active in a whole range of private organizations concerned with infants' and women's health. This team brought to the task of setting up the school medical service a range of diverse experiences and expertise: in Jane Greig's own words, 'one, a Rhodes scholar, was a children's specialist and a research student in physiology, another was an educationalist and experienced lecturer, and the third had given special attention to the diseases of women and children and to public health'.[19]

It was Greig whose main interests were in the field of public health, and she was the first woman to receive the Diploma of Public Health from the University of Melbourne in 1910. She was also active in a wide range of organizations concerned with the promotion of women's health and baby welfare.[20] While all three medical officers were celebrants of scientific medicine, interest in school anthropometrics and feeble-mindedness were brought to their project particularly by Mary Booth and Harvey Sutton. Booth had been an anthropometrist with the Department of the Government Statist, a position she held for four years from 1900, before entering the Victorian Department of Public Instruction in 1904 as a lecturer in hygiene and later, in 1909, as a medical officer.[21] She was reputedly fiercely patriotic and strongly feminist, and later in her career raised funds for a publication, *The Boy Settler*, as a means of maintaining the purity of British stock in Australia and combating communism. Sutton, the Rhodes scholar, had already achieved some distinction as a doctor and medical researcher by the time he took up his position in the Department of Public Instruction.[22] While he was some ten years the junior of Greig and fourteen years younger than Booth, he seems to have taken a leading role in the group, at least in terms of mapping out their scheme of work. In addition to their diverse specialisms, each of the medical officers had a keen interest in eugenics.

All three had affiliations with official eugenics organizations, with Booth as we have seen developing the AAAS's rationale for a national anthropometric survey and Greig and Sutton helping to form the provisional committee of the Eugenics Education Society of Melbourne, established in July 1914.[23]

Bringing this range of interests to bear on the task of establishing the school medical service in Victoria, the collection of data on children's growth and development, as well as their various ailments and afflictions, was a central feature of the school medical service's work. Detailed anthropometric measurements were made during the first years of the service. In a retrospective account of the early years of the medical service written in 1921, Jane Greig suggested that initially not everyone was in favour of the inclusion of anthropometric testing and that it prompted 'keen discussion'. The main concern was that such surveys could be rendered useless through insufficient care and lack of uniform standards. Greig wrote that the school medical officers were aware that the measurements 'would be valuable in proportion to the care with which they were done and that . . . they must be carefully standardised so that they would be valuable for comparison both with those of the Commonwealth and with those of other countries'. Despite these initial concerns, anthropometric testing was included as an integral part of medical inspection in Victoria, with the medical officers extremely interested in the results it might yield since 'so little information existed in regard to the normal Australian child and as tens of thousands of children would soon come under review, it was felt that a great opportunity would be missed if some observations of this kind were not made'.[24]

Booth, Greig and Sutton's first report, for the 1909–10 school year, extensively and impressively mapped out the boundaries of what the medical officers perceived to be the school medical service's responsibilities, including definitions and qualifications of their activities, and proposals for future work. In the process, the three medical officers identified a number of key functions: the medical examination of students and teachers, and the systematic recording of information on medical and dental condition, growth and factors retarding physical development, and racial origins; prognosis and prescription of treatment of defectives; in-service training of teachers to be equipped to include hygiene as a curriculum topic; and advice on the suitability of school buildings and playgrounds. All of this work was predicated ostensibly on the assumption that there was a relationship between the health of children and their educational attainment.

> In many cases we get the formation of a vicious circle; a child with a
> defect becomes, as a result of such defect, unable to take in what is told
> him, and, in the effort to overcome the handicap, suffers overstrain.
> The work that suits the average of the class is too much, so that the
> fatigue limit is transgressed, the pace has become too fast, and the

> result is that he falls back and makes no progress. The defects, for example, astigmatism, short sight, &c., are accentuated by this effort, with further bad effect on the child . . . . The removal of the defect breaks through this circle, oftentimes with the happiest results . . . . The more completely these defects are eliminated from our school population, the more rapid and real, we may presume, will be the progress of the pupils, and the easier and more effective the efforts of the teacher.[25]

The fact that articulation of this relationship between medical inspection, the child's well-being and educational achievement appears fifteen pages in to the report rather than at the beginning suggests that the effectiveness of instruction in the government schools of Victoria was not the overriding motivation for the establishment and development of the medical officers' scheme of work. Questions of racial deterioration and economic productivity seem to have figured large in the inauguration of a school medical service in Victoria. The Victorian government, alarmed at the medical officers' initial findings, viewed the work of the school medical service in the most serious light: 'If it is true that the production of efficient citizens and the physical, as well as mental and moral, progress of a people is very greatly affected, if not largely controlled, by the healthy training and development of its children, then the work of medical inspection and school hygiene must be regarded as being of national importance'.[26] On the basis of this view, the school medical service in Victoria was intended to meet both the immediate problems of instructional effectiveness in schools and the related question of the supply of a productive citizenry. In the medical officers' own terms, 'the child is the main asset of the nation. He, and not the often doubtful product from across the seas, is our best immigrant. Rightly used, we believe that "the periodical stocktaking of the child-life of our community", which medical inspection represents, may be a most important factor in our national welfare'.[27]

The eugenicist flavour of these statements is clear, and the influence of eugenics is reflected in the medical officers' elaboration of their programme. The rationale which underpinned advocacy for a national anthropometric survey was integral to the Victorian school medical service's programme from the start. Where variations in the Anglo-Celtic stock were detected, Booth, Greig and Sutton suggested in their first report that those individuals and groups disadvantageous to the progeniture of a productive citizenry need to be 'counteracted with intelligent care'. Preventative medicine was, in their view, the key means of acting on such comparisons, since 'it is not at present permissible to control parentage'. Thus, they argued, 'the health and development of the human product and the control of his environment are matters very much at our disposal'. The setting of standards derived from systematic measurements of children's health, growth and physical as well as moral development were the means by which such control could properly be achieved.[28]

Sutton's contribution to this argument was further elaborated in a section of the first report dealing with 'the backward and feeble-minded'.[29] While there can be no doubt that compassion for these children inspired Sutton's interest in this problem, his concern to seek a solution in the gradual diminution of numbers suffering from 'congenital imperfection' was largely inspired by eugenics. Both in the 1909–10 report and in a 1913 lecture given in the Australian Church Lecture Hall in Melbourne, Sutton argued that the systematic study of the laws of heredity could, with 'almost mathematical exactness',[30] lead to the eradication of the 'low-type of a man' invariably found to be 'idiots, lunatics, unemployables, habitual criminals, cripples from birth'.[31] The medical officers considered detection of such children and advice on their care and treatment to be their primary task, but at the same time they set about collecting detailed quantitative information on their nationality and race, parents' occupations and family history of diseases such as 'tuberculosis, rheumatism, nervous and heart disease' of the school children they examined.[32]

Over the next five years, until Sutton's departure to join the war effort reduced the service's staff, the medical officers put their plans into action, reporting in precise and intricate detail the results of their examinations of schoolboys and schoolgirls in Victoria. The Minister of Public Instruction Reports for the years between 1909 and 1915 contain tabulated and graphed information on all manner of physical ailment. In addition to listing the numbers of children examined, organized by sex, age ranges and types of schools, the medical officers detailed numbers of children suffering from defects of vision, hearing, nose and throat, hair, teeth, physical deformity, and major organs. Heights and weights were recorded, along with nationality of parents and grandparents, information on the percentage of Australian, British and other racial ingredient being presented according to the scheme outlined in Sutton's paper on 'The importance of nationality'.[33] The anthropometric measurement of teachers was included in the Minister of Public Instruction Report for 1914–15, and special sections devoted to 'The growth of the Australian child' and 'Immigrants' appeared in the 1912–13 and the 1914–15 Reports respectively.[34]

By their 1914–15 report to the government, the last before Sutton's departure, the regulatory imperative underpinning the task of school medical inspection was increasingly in evidence. In this report, the medical officers provided a table of measurements of immigrant children, mostly from Britain, which could be compared with Australian-born children, including measurements of height, weight, chest and head. They suggested that 'the association of light eyes (blue eyes) with certain mental characteristics [is] pointed out as the result of observations among Victorian children. The marked preponderance of the blue-eyed in rural districts and the corresponding dominance of the brown-eyed in centers of population were shown, and attributed to the enterprising character of the blue-eyed in seeking a field for scope for their activities'.[35] On the basis of such comparisons between urban, suburban and rural children, Sutton was prepared to generalize that the cleanliness of children from the industrial centres at some distance from the sea was poorest, while the nutrition of children in country towns was best. In terms of physique, 'the very finest specimens . . . have been found among the students engaged in agricultural work'.[36]

In making such statements, Sutton undoubtedly believed himself to be drawing on the data he and the others had collected. However, it is clear that his extrapolations beyond this data were shaped by some of the stock notions of the time concerning the wholesomeness of the rural setting versus the degeneracy of urban life, which in turn gave substance to the normative and regulatory activities implicit in school medical inspection. The literary stereotypes of Banjo Paterson and the homunculi of Marcus Clarke's[37] imagination were reconstructed by the Victorian school medical officers on the basis of what they believed to be scientific fact. Robust physique was equated with slow but dependable intelligence to be found mainly in rural areas, whereas urban dwellers were quick-witted but physically degenerate.

In the country towns remote from the railways the children are as a rule not 'smart'. They are somewhat slow to learn; but there is ample compensation for this in the tenacity with which they retain what they are taught. Both boys and girls in such localities are rather solid in physique, and of good general health. A thickly populated suburb shows a contrast. The children generally are more alert. Quick to learn, often they are equally quick to forget. Occasionally a child of singular precocity is found in a place of this kind; but in such a case there is likely to be a pathetic loss of brightness and a decline in intellectual capacity at an early age. Children in a neighborhood of this description are usually less robust in build than country children.[38]

While their anthropometric measurements may have indicated differences in cleanliness and physique between urban and rural children, such attempts to equate them with temperament and intellectual capacity were pure fiction, shaped as much by the prevailing mythologies of Australian identity developing during the closing decades of the nineteenth century as by the data they had collected. Geoffrey Dutton has pointed out that, in the first decade of the twentieth century, 'country life was harder, dirtier (if only because there was often no water to wash in) and more hazardous than city life'.[39] This contrasting assessment at least calls into question the impartiality of the medical officers' investigations; they certainly seemed eager to find confirmation in their data of the prevailing Eurocentric wisdom of the day, that physical and moral degeneracy was most likely to be found in the urban setting. More to the point, the data collected was itself shaped by these myths and cultural stereotypes. By 1915, the medical officers' recordings of eye colour and assorted other physical features, along with findings of anthropometric and mental testing, were proposed as a basis for the development of criteria to guide the selection of immigrants. Blue eyes, clean skin and robust physique were in, brown eyes, dirt and physical frailty were out.

In contrast to the rather severe implications of this kind of work for some sections of the population, medical inspection received very generous attention from the popular press in the early years. Inspection was portrayed as of major social consequence, with its normative dimension assumed to be natural, benign and humanitarian. The first medical inspections in Melbourne schools were reported in light-hearted detail by the *Argus*.

> In a little room, the office, at the Graham-street State school, Port Melbourne, yesterday, four or five boys, stripped to the waist, were waiting to see the doctor. It was the opening of the Education department's scheme for the medical inspection of State school children. In the office, Dr. Harvey Sutton, with the headmaster Mr. B. Richards, assisting in the clerical work, was making a systematic examination of the boys; in a classroom Drs. Mary Booth and Jean Greig were inspecting the girls; and in a shed in the morning, four members of the Odontological Society, acting in an honorary capacity, were examining the teeth of the scholars. So much cheerfulness pervaded the office, where boys stripped off shirts and flannels to reveal brown skins, that it was difficult to realise that the lads were on a visit to the doctor. A boy knocked at the door, and at the summons 'come in', he shyly turned the handle and looked in. His face was set with appropriate seriousness, but as soon as he saw his schoolmates comfortably dangling their legs on long stools, or regarding with interest curious instruments, which did not look as fearful as instruments of a more homely nature, his features relaxed, and he was a confident small boy again. Then he looked into the smiling eyes of a big, broad young man with curly hair, and the idea took root in his mind that he would like to visit the doctor everyday.[40]

Propaganda of this kind was necessary since a range of parties including, as we will see in the next chapter, parents and the medical profession, did not share either the medical officers' or the state governments' conviction that the state's intervention in this delicate business of examining children's

63

bodies was an appropriate way to proceed. When we consider some of the interpretations of their data Sutton and his colleagues were prepared to make, we might conclude that these reservations were not without foundation.

Examined Bodies

With the benefit of hindsight and the work of Foucault, we can characterize school anthropometry and medical inspection broadly as an attempt to normalize children's bodies. The identification of defects and the consequent definition of normality effectively constructed and constituted Australians as white, able-bodied, socially and morally disciplined, and economically productive or, in the case of women, biologically reproductive. While this encoding of physical normality took place primarily within the discourse of school medical inspection, the positioning of many children as physically defective would also have played a part in the formation of their subjective self-awareness.

Given their overwhelming concern for race, it is significant that very little attention was paid to Aboriginal children in the medical officers' stock-taking reports, apart from occasional inspections. The medical officers seemed to believe that Aboriginal children's health could, like that of Anglo-Celtic children, be improved through medical inspection. But one possible implication of the omission of data on the indigenous population is that their bodies were considered too different from white bodies to be normalized. Within the normalizing discourse of school medical inspection, Aboriginal bodies could only be 'other' to the 'Australian' bodies of white Anglo-Celts.

A relatively literal reading of the discourse of school medical inspection and anthropometrics during the period immediately preceding and following the First World War leaves little doubt that these eugenics-inspired practices were part of a configuration of practices including epidemiological surveys, social medicine and public health practices aimed at what Bryan Turner has described as 'a policing of populations and a clinic of bodies'.[41] Indeed, allied to the national system of physical training established in 1911 by the Commonwealth Department of Defence and carried out under the auspices of the Junior Cadet Training Scheme, school anthropometrics and medical inspection presented a potentially powerful set of normalizing practices that produced examined bodies.

A literal reading of the discourse of medical inspection by itself could be dangerously misleading, however, since it might present too seamless a process of normalization and regulation. Set beside the various sources of resistance to the scheme from the British Medical Association of Australia and parents, the structural imperfections of the medical services themselves including shortage of funds to employ suitable numbers of doctors and their inability to treat defects, and the events of the First World War and its aftermath, we are forced to examine critically the school medical officers' attempts to contribute to the evolution of a robust white Australian race in the southern hemisphere. In the next chapter, we assess the extent to which school medical inspection and physical training together may have made a successful contribution to schooling bodies during and following the First World War.

Notes and References

1 Foucault, M. (1977) *Discipline and Punish: The Birth of the Prison* New York: Allen & Unwin, pp. 184–5.
2 Wood, T.D. and Rowell, H.G. (1927) *Health Supervision and Medical Inspection of Schools* Philadelphia: W.B. Saunders.
3 Cf. Smith, W.D. (1974) *Stretching Their Bodies: The History of Physical Education* London: David & Charles, pp. 96–101.
4 Board of Education/Scottish Education Department (1903) *Royal Commission on Physical Training (Scotland)* London: HMSO.
5 Thompson, I. (1978) The origins of physical education in state schools *Scottish Educational Review*, **10** (2), pp. 17–34.
6 Hogarth, A.H. (1909) *Medical Inspection of Schools* London: Hodder & Stoughton, p. 41.
7 Coghlan, T.A. (1902) Child measurement. *Australasian Association for the Advancement of Science (AAAS) Conference Proceedings*, pp. 543–5.
8 *Australian Dictionary of Biography*, **7**, 1891–1939, p. 300.
9 Bjelke-Petersen, H.-C. (1902) Growth and development of Hobart schoolboys with some notes on anthropometry *AAAS Conference Proceedings*, p. 823.
10 Bjelke-Petersen, Growth and development of Hobart schoolboys, p. 828.
11 Booth, M. (1911) School anthropometrics *AAAS Conference Proceedings*, pp. 689–95.
12 Booth, School anthropometrics, p. 695
13 Sutton, H. (1911) The importance of nationality *AAAS Conference Proceedings*, p. 509.
14 Sutton, The importance of nationality, p. 510.
15 Sutton, H. (1912) *Australian Medical Conference Proceedings*, p. 51.
16 *AAAS Conference Proceedings*, 1921, pp. 355–56.
17 *AAAS Conference Proceedings*, 1923, p. xlvi.
18 Medical inspection and treatment of school children *Medical Journal of Australia*, 25 July 1914, p. 83.
19 Greig, J. (1921) School medical inspection in Victoria *Medical Journal of Australia*, 30 April, pp. 361–62.
20 *Australian Dictionary of Biography (ADB) 1901-1939*, **9**, p. 102.
21 *ADB 1901–1939*, **7**, pp. 345–6.
22 *ADB 1901–1939*, **12**, pp. 143–4.
23 *Argus*, 14 July, 1914, p. 11.
24 Greig, School medical inspection, p. 362.

25 Minister of Public Instruction (1910) *Education Report for the Year 1909–10* Melbourne: Government Printer, p. 110.

26 Minister of Public Instruction Report, 1910, p. 22.

27 Minister of Public Instruction Report, 1910, p. 97.

28 Minister of Public Instruction Report, 1910, pp. 96–109.

29 Minister of Public Instruction Report, 1910, pp. 107–8.

30 Sutton, H. (1913) The cure of feeble-mindedness *Australasian Medical Gazette,* 7 June, p. 556.

31 Minister of Public Instruction Report, 1910, p. 107.

32 Minister of Public Instruction Report, 1910, p. 114.

33 Sutton, The importance of nationality, pp. 508–10.

34 Minister of Public Instruction (1915) *Education Report for the Year 1914–1915* Melbourne: Government Printer, pp. 87–90; Minister of Public Instruction (1913) *Education Report for the Year 1912–1913* Melbourne: Government Printer, pp. 119–22.

35 Minister of Public Instruction Report, 1915, pp. 89–90.

36 *Argus*, 10 May 1911.

37 Clark, M. (1877) *The Future Australian Race* Melbourne: A.H. Massina & Co.

38 *Argus*, 10 May 1911.

39 Dutton, G. (1971) *Australia Since the Camera: From Federation to War 1901–1914* Melbourne: Cheshire.

40 State school children – first medical inspection *Argus*, 16 February 1910.

41 Turner, B.S. (1984) *The Body and Society: Explorations in Social Theory* Oxford: Blackwell, p. 50.

4

Resisting Bodies: Physical Training and Medical Inspection in Decline

Any system of defence which asks for drill alone or mainly drill as a duty will, whether the appeal is to man or boy, be a failure. Considered even as a preparation for impending battle, drill may quite easily be overvalued. It was not drill that gave the name Anzac its immortal meaning. It was an exceptional moral courage born of sunshine, a free life, education, a fine national pride, but above and beyond all – supreme physical fitness.[1]

We do . . . object to the perfunctory system of the 'march past' which led one of the inspectors, to her everlasting honor, to resign rather than be a party to it . . . . We do object to the magnification of figures by the inclusion of trifling and negligible defects which we know is done. . . We object to so-called statistics being published under official authority and warranty, and sent all over the world, professing to show that from 70% to 80% of our school children suffer physical defects. It is an exaggeration and a libel on Australians.[2]

The regular medical inspection of school children was established in most Australian states by the end of the first decade of the century, while the national system of physical training under the auspices of the Junior Cadet Training Scheme officially came into operation in 1911. Both sets of practices were embedded in the interconnecting public discourses of nationalism and militarism, race deterioration and public health, economic productivity and social order and were directed emphatically at schooling bodies. There existed tensions between support for physical training on the grounds of military training and social order in contrast to concerns to improve the health of school children, a goal that was also at odds with the eugenicist desire to use medical inspection to minimize the reproduction of 'defectives'. Notwithstanding these tensions, physical training and school medical inspection can be regarded as complementary technologies of power concerned with the regulation and normalization of children's bodies. Each set of practices shared a concern to work in meticulous and precise fashion on children's bodies, drilling children's movements in space and in time, examining, measuring and recording in minute detail their physical characteristics.

Both schemes attracted a mixed reception of support and opposition during their first years of operation, as might be expected of any innovation. While some of the opposition became vociferous, this criticism did little at first to divert the course of policy implementation. However, neither critics nor supporters could have been prepared for the dramatic shift in public discourse that was to accompany Australia's involvement in the First World War, particularly after 1915 when the full horror of modern warfare began to confront the public. Suddenly, there were new metaphors to describe Australian national identity, the desire to turn boys into junior soldiers seemed less benign, and the detailed mapping of children's defects seemed to be petty and unnecessarily negative.

In a very short space of time, the discourses that provided militarized physical training and eugenics-inspired school medical inspection with legitimacy underwent a dramatic change that robbed these school practices of much of their social relevance. This chapter describes the first few years of each scheme in operation before the coming storm of world war, and then shows how these technologies of power were fatally undermined before they could become effective means of regulating the bodies of school children. The changing circumstances in which physical training and school medical inspection were practised facilitated the resistance of children, their parents, and other parties to these attempts to school bodies, even though this resistance fell far short of a collective or coherent opposition to corporeal regulation.

Militarized Physical Training:
The First Years of the Scheme in Operation

Of all the states, Victoria seems to have embraced the Junior Cadet Training Scheme with greatest enthusiasm, with Frank Tate, the Director of Education, having been personally involved in both Melbourne conferences. In 1912, the Victorian Minister of Public Instruction was prepared to state that:

Already the good effect of the drill is noticeable in many schools, in the better carriage of the scholars, and in the improved bodily positions adopted by the scholar during ordinary school lessons. The organized

games are tending not only to increase the play movements, but also
to induce a better kind of exercising play for all the children . . . .
Means will be taken, during next year, to ascertain, by examination
and measurement of scholars, the developmental effect of the new
physical training. The physical well-being of the children is receiving
careful attention from the officers and teachers of the Department.[3]

After only one year of operation, this was rather an optimistic view.
Nevertheless, this statement does indicate that there was enthusiasm and
support for the new scheme in some quarters. In particular, Frank Tate's
considerable investment of time and energy in helping set up the scheme,
his well-known commitment to 'national efficiency' and his conviction
that government should avoid duplication of effort and resources,
accounted for at least some of Victoria's supportive posture. The general
public were kept informed of developments by the press, who also seemed
to be taking an enthusiastic and supportive view of the new scheme. The
Argus reported on the issue frequently and at some length, mostly in a
celebratory tone.

Australia's future men and women should form a sturdy race when
the ideals aimed at under the Defence Act are fully realised. The
compulsory service system has been in operation somewhat less than
two years, but already its beneficial effect is being shown, since, as a
direct result of fifteen minutes every day, the majority of the 609,000
children – both boys and girls – who attend schools throughout
Australia now receive scientific instruction in physical exercises. Not
only are the scholars taught to perform set movements with hands and
feet, which are usually associated with what might be described as
'bathroom' gymnastics, but great attention is also devoted to marching
evolutions (some of which assume at later stages almost the involved
movements of the ballet).[4]

If the *Argus*'s reporter Donald Macdonald is to be believed, the training
courses for male and female teachers organized during the summer vacation
of 1912 were stimulating and reasonably pleasant affairs. Indeed, the
teachers attended on a voluntary basis and bore most of the costs themselves.[5] At the camp for males in Geelong, 140 students were drilled with
military discipline, though according to Macdonald, not without humour
and tact: 'the man who drilled them on routine lines, making it pure drudgery, would have them resentful in next to no time'. Harvey Sutton, Director
of the school medical service in Victoria, supplemented the physical and
military drill with lectures on hygiene, physiology and body mechanics,
while the champion swimmer Frank Beaurepaire, only recently appointed

Organiser of Swimming for Victorian schools, took morning and evening classes.

The women, on the other hand, were drilled 'just enough . . . to facilitate falling in and forming squads'. Housed three miles from the men at Osborne House, 130 female teachers were instructed by Gertrude Anderson in the arts of physical exercises and folk dancing, while May Cox, the female Organiser of Swimming in Victoria, taught dry-land swimming in a tree-lined sunken garden, since the beach at Osborne House was unsuitable for bathing. The sight of the women teachers in 'rational costume' was obviously something of a novelty for Macdonald. With some delicacy he explained that 'without the least strain on chivalry one may describe this assemblage of teachers as distinctly dainty. Their physical culture costumes, in which they spend the greater part of the day, are decidedly dainty, and rational, but not at all in a weird way. They wear short tunics and knickers, dark blue, and white rubber shoes. In hats alone there is no uniformity – the most serviceable perhaps for all purposes being the white twill.'

These idyllic scenes penned by Macdonald provide a clear illustration of the ways in which schooling bodies was deeply implicated in the construction of gender. Even within a scheme of militarized physical training that is framed within a discourse of masculinity, firm distinctions were drawn between appropriate activities and forms of dress for males and females. Women were drilled 'just enough', while men were drilled with 'military discipline', and these activities were not permitted to detract from a view of women as 'dainty' creatures. Macdonald fails to mention the men's attire, but is compelled to write in some detail about the women's appearance.

The scenes may have appeared idyllic, but they did not tell the whole story. The other state education departments did not share Victoria's apparently uncritical acceptance of and enthusiasm for the new scheme, and in July 1912 yet another Conference on Physical Training was convened by representatives of the state education departments to consider 'the progress and future of physical and other Junior cadet training'.[6] On this occasion, significantly, Tate was not present, though the Directors of Education for New South Wales, South Australia and Tasmania were. Victoria was represented by an Inspector of Schools, and this time Queensland also sent a representative.

This Conference's main concern was to reduce the number of hours required for cadet training from 120 to 90, a request that the Defence Department subsequently accepted.[7] There was some continuing bickering over financial matters: who, for instance, should pay the cost of postage incurred by Education Departments in connection with the scheme. The Defence Department agreed to foot the bill. The military also agreed to reduce the number of elective activities from two to one, but refused to accede to the Conference's request to eliminate miniature rifle shooting altogether.

By the middle of 1913, some 1200 male teachers nationally had satisfactorily completed the course of instruction offered by the Defence Department physical training staff for the Certificate of Physical Training.[8] By 1915, the total number of certificated teachers had risen to two and a half thousand in Victoria alone.[9] In addition, male teachers from all over the country 'who show more than the ordinary aptitude' for cadet training were receiving advanced level training from 1913.[10] The Education Departments' insistence that girls also be catered for within the scheme required the training of instructresses, since it was felt that it would be quite improper for the army's physical training instructors to train women teachers, confirming again that physical training was deeply concerned with gender construction.[11]

Initially, the Director of Physical Training Bjelke-Petersen argued against what he perceived to be corner-cutting on the part of the states in suggesting that women who were qualified to teach cadets in addition to girls and younger boys were also qualified to train female teachers, and he suggested that 'the growing womanhood of Australia' was being short-changed by their hurry to put a comprehensive system in place.[12] His protests were in vain. Over April and May 1913, Major Alderson, Chief Instructor of the Physical Training Staff, ran a five-week course in Melbourne for women organizers and assistants who would conduct this training of women teachers. Twenty-two women attended the instructress's course, including Gertrude Anderson from Victoria, Ella Gormley from New South Wales, Miss L. Mills from Western Australia and two Queenslanders, Misses J. Lang and E. Henry. Their course included classes in chemistry, physiology, hygiene, physical training, organized games, marching drill, and practical teaching in metropolitan schools made available by Frank Tate.[13]

Besides the ongoing undertone of suspicion and distrust which exuded from some of the state education departments, the scheme soon ran into opposition in other quarters. At their conference in March 1913, ministers of the Methodist churches of Victoria and Tasmania attacked the compulsory military training system, claiming that it was the nearest thing to conscription and that the method of its establishment had been undemocratic.[14] The Presbyterians were equally divided at their General Assembly held in May of the same year.[15] The Reverend Dr John Burgess argued that 'the scheme is conscription, for the essential element is in compulsion', and put a motion that the Assembly express its disapproval of compulsory classes in military training. While the motion received a seconder, it was not supported after what was described, in admirable understatement by the newspaper reporter, as a 'warm discussion'.

The compulsory nature of the scheme was not to be taken lightly, as many so-called 'drill shirkers' found to their cost. During the first year of the scheme, defaulters were treated relatively leniently. From the middle of

1912, however, prosecutions began in earnest.[16] Although magistrates varied in the severity of their sentencing, the compulsory nature of the scheme attracted growing, though patchily reported, criticism, with the *Argus* admitting that it could not publish the volume of letters it received on the subject.[17] In one case, over 40 cadets were summoned to appear before a magistrate in Sydney for failing to perform the requisite number of drills under the Defence Act, with over 30 being confined to barracks for up to ten days, and some ordered to pay costs.[18] In the first two years of the scheme alone, over twelve thousand defaulting junior and senior cadets were prosecuted.[19]

Prime Minister Andrew Fisher himself had more than a taste of the opposition to the scheme. On a fine Saturday in May 1913, he was confronted in Adelaide by a large and angry deputation of women representing the Young Women's Christian Association, the Seventh Day Adventists and the Women's Christian Temperance Movement.[20] Fisher's attempts to explain his position were subject to frequent interjections and dissent from the women. Through the uproar, he was reported to have claimed that he knew the scheme was not perfect, but it was the best means available for the defence of the country. For his trouble, the women responded that he had 'the motherhood of the country' against him. Fisher was left in no doubt that whatever the benefits to the school-age population at large in terms of physical training, it was the compulsory nature of the military training which provoked such angry resentment.[21]

Militarized Physical Training in Decline: The First World War and Its Aftermath

There is considerable irony and, perhaps, more than a little poetic justice in the fact that the First World War had a disastrous effect on this scheme of compulsory military training. The war severely restricted the operation of the scheme before it had a chance to become established. Indeed, according to Kitchener's advice, the scheme was not scheduled to be at full strength until 1919.[22] The enlistment of male teachers in growing numbers through 1915 and 1916 decimated the cadet units, and left the organization of physical training for both girls and boys in the hands of female teachers.[23] The carnage of the war, the sheer extent of the loss of Australian lives, and the growing anti-war sentiments that were aroused among the general public now left physical training with the distinct disadvantage of being associated with military training. As early as April 1917, the Anzac legend was being cited by Donald Macdonald of the *Argus* as an argument against compulsory military training of the kind required by the Junior Cadet Training Scheme.

What the founders of the compulsory system failed to realise is that with boys discipline is something to coax and encourage rather than to command, that the coaxing is made doubly difficult in being coupled with a monotonous duty; so instead of self-discipline, the really desirable end, the system gives nothing but resentful and grudging obedience . . . . In brief, the outstanding defect of the system is that it offers the boy no interest, nothing in games or competitions that appeal to youth.[24]

Macdonald argued that to attempt to command obedience rather than earn it was unAustralian and doomed to failure. This sort of criticism certainly struck a chord and provides evidence of a profound shift in public discourse as a result of the war. As Geoffrey Searle[25] pointed out, before the war had ended the digger had already become a second idealized Australian type alongside the bushman, his spectacular success as a soldier due, it was argued, to his membership of 'the democratic army of one of the most democratic peoples the world had seen who were characterised above all by social equality'. The Australian soldier's legendary lack of respect for rank and discipline was, according to General Monash, 'misunderstood . . . in the Australian forces no strong insistence was ever made upon the mere outward form of discipline . . . the Australian Army is a proof that individualism is the best and not the worst foundation upon which to build collective discipline'. If Macdonald's observations were accurate, then the successes of the Australian Imperial Force during the war owed much to the failures of this form of military and physical training to suppress Australian individualism.[26]

This change in the public discourse of nationalism and its relationship to militarism made it easier to criticize the Junior Cadet Scheme and physical training more openly. In 1919, now former Director of Physical Training Bjelke-Petersen was highly critical of the general standard of work in schools and what he perceived to be unrealistic expectations placed on ill-prepared teachers to raise physical training above the level of drudgery. After touring Queensland he commented: 'it was very noticeable that teaching had a tendency to become mechanical. The teachers gave just the words of command and the explanations from the syllabus without teaching points and without aiming at putting in that delightful spice of variety and original remarks.'[27]

Bjelke-Petersen's report also revealed that in the opinions of some educationalists the fears expressed at the early Melbourne conferences had been realized and military instructors were employing methods inappropriate to school children. In his report, he cited remarks made by a senior teacher in the Tasmanian Education Department that:

Our universal training had not really been a success because our instructors do not understand the material they have to develop and get into shape, namely, boys. They seem to think that methods suitable when handling grown men who have to be trained quickly for military purposes, are suitable for boys . . . . We must get [the military instructors] to understand the psychology of interest and the physiological requirements for varied activity which exists in the minds of growing boys and not allow our instructors to use the set formal methods used with adults.

In the face of the kind of criticism reflected in Macdonald's article and in Bjelke-Petersen's report, there were attempts to broaden the range of activities within the scheme in ways which might 'appeal to youth'.[28] In 1915, Rosalie Virtue became female Organiser of Physical Training in Victoria and, in the absence of her male colleagues, gained an important foothold during the war for alternative forms of physical training. By the early 1920s, she was recommending the use of modified exercises and methods of training for infants and girls, including greater use of games and rhythmic activities performed to music. Virtue's work with girls offered a clear alternative to militaristic physical training, with the developing female tradition in England based on the therapeutic values of Swedish gymnastics providing a continuing source of ideas and inspiration.[29] Her work not only offered girls a genuine and legitimate alternative to the formality of physical training; as we will see in Chapter 6, it was to form the foundation of a new, liberalized physical education for both girls and boys which flourished in the decades following the Second World War.

The states were evidently increasingly keen to make use of the physical training component of the cadet scheme for their own educational and related purposes, while taking the military training aspect on sufferance. Despite the considerable advantages they continued to enjoy with respect to the training of their teachers and the instruction of their senior boys in the cadet scheme, they were loath to pay for any of these services. When the Minister of State for Defence announced in September 1920 that the time had arrived for consideration of the scheme being taken over by the states, the Directors of Education convened a hasty meeting to fight the proposal that they should bear the cost of the enterprise.[30] A resolution could not be reached, however, and the Defence Department's responsibilities for junior cadet training ceased in June 1922. The states, ill-prepared for such a sudden withdrawal of Commonwealth beneficence, persisted in their protests to such an extent that they persuaded the federal government to reinstate the scheme in July 1924, though with a leaner budget and in a streamlined form. But this was merely delaying the inevitable. For the next five years, the Junior Cadet Training Scheme stumbled along under constant threat of further cost-cutting[31] and with low morale until, in November 1929, the Prime Minister announced the suspension of the entire compulsory military training scheme.[32]

The economic argument was clearly the overriding one for the government (even though Prime Minister Scullin attempted to play to both sides of the issue by claiming to support defence and general disarmament), the Commonwealth estimating that they would save £180,000 in the 1929 financial year by suspending compulsory military training.[33] The suspension of the scheme roused strong sentiments. In most cases, it was the loss of the system of physical, rather than military, training which prompted statements of protest.[34] Reflecting this theme, one contributor to the debate suggested the replacement of compulsory military training with compulsory physical training, which would at least maintain a high level of national fitness, and which might satisfy both the supporters of cadet training and those pacifists who opposed militarism.[35] It was clearly too late for constructive suggestions, however enterprising or conciliatory, since the government had decided that the money needed to run any kind of national training scheme was simply not available.

The military, as might have been expected, were particularly outspoken over the Labour government's alleged short-sightedness in hastily removing compulsory military training without a ready replacement. Lieutenant-General Sir Harry Chauvel expressed 'grave doubts' concerning the wisdom of the government's decision, and recalled his repeated references to the weaknesses of Australia's defences.[36] During the period of temporary suspension of the scheme, the four-year contracts of all Defence Department physical training staff were cancelled and replaced by employment on a fortnightly basis. Now Director of Physical Training and a Lieutenant-Colonel, Alderson claimed that the entire range of work of the instructors was in jeopardy, not merely the work in schools.[37] He refuted the suggestion that the staff should be transferred to the state education departments on the grounds that the arguments against such an arrangement had been soundly and conclusively put in 1922. He had no sympathy, either, for the view that they might come under the control of the Department of Public Health, as was the arrangement in England. He was particularly scathing of this proposal, claiming that the argument was made without analysis of the actual needs of Australians whose 'physique is of a high standard . . . climatic conditions aid natural development and there is not the need for the practice of remedial exercises so necessary in some of the older countries with confined localities and difficult living conditions'. Alderson had been an advocate of closer cooperation between the Defence Force staff and the school medical services in relation to the physical development of school children,[38] but this apparent goodwill between the physical training instructors and school medical personnel clearly did not amount to a desire to work under their supervision.

Cutting off these last routes of escape for the physical training staff may not have been a wise move, given that they were threatened with extinction. What was initially proposed as a temporary suspension was still in place when the Scullin government fell in December 1931, though by this time the Commonwealth had completely withdrawn its support for the Junior Cadet Training Scheme. The state education departments were once again caught out by the withdrawal of support for physical training in schools.[39] While there was general regret at the loss of physical training, there were few supporters of a continuation of military training and no takers for the Defence Department's physical training staff.

School Medical Inspection:
Resistance to the Scheme in Operation

In the early years of medical inspection in Victorian schools Booth, Greig and Sutton spent considerable time and effort securing the willing coopera-tion of teachers and parents. They attended meetings held at the schools to explain their work and to offer advice on hygiene and other health matters arising from their inspections of children which, it was claimed, 'are always well attended and the questions asked show that the work of the officers is being keenly watched and fully appreciated'.[40] This expenditure of effort seems to have been necessary, since not everyone was convinced that school medical inspection was prompted solely by humanitarian concerns.

The medical officers were well aware that the success of school medical inspection depended on the cooperation of parents. It was they who filled out the cards that provided the medical officers with pupils' medical histories and, if a defect was identified, it was the parents who sought treatment for their child. The Acts that established the school medical service in Victoria and the other states enabled the practice of medical inspection, but did not make treatment obligatory, and the medical officers were not permitted to treat the children they examined.[41] Restrictions on the treatment of pupils was a matter of some frustration to Booth, Greig and Sutton; they could identify physical defects and make recommendations regarding treatment for individual children and for school hygiene, but they could not ensure that treatment took place, nor could they change the home environment.

By 1915, it had emerged from the Victorian school medical officers' investigations that over 33 per cent of children found to have defects had not officially received treatment.[42] Some members of the medical profession preferred to see this as an indication of parental irresponsibility.[43] However, among the poorer sections of the community in particular, a visit to the doctor meant considerable expense. Consequently, many Australians preferred to treat themselves and their children, and provided a rich market for patent medicines. There was also great faith in home remedies and cures.[44] If a medical problem seemed beyond parental expertise the local chemist was often consulted before a doctor, simply because the chemist was cheaper and more accessible. In the opinion of many parents such remedies constituted effective treatment.

It was within this context that the *Argus* could report as early as August 1911 that there was a 'feeling of resentment' amongst the parents of children attending Shepparton state and high schools on being required to fill in a card containing a series of 29 questions.[45] The questions were framed, according to another report, with 'the object of ascertaining the occupation and nationality of parents; the family history, so that hereditary disease might be guarded against; the progress of infancy, so that previous illnesses might be recorded'.[46] Other parents expressed their refusal to take the role of the school medical officer too seriously in their reply to questions; when asked had their son ever suffered from indigestion, one parent replied 'Yes, after a picnic.' Lack of cooperation on the part of parents was to persist into the 1920s, with many continuing, through 'lack of interest', 'fear' or 'poverty' to defy the medical officers' recommendations for treatment of their children, while others voiced their strong opposition to answering questions about their children's nationality and racial origins.[47]

During the first five years of the service, between 1909 and 1913, Mary Booth resigned to be replaced by Eileen Fitzgerald, and C.J. Simpson was appointed to assist with the added responsibility of the medical examination of teachers. By 1914, this group of four had documented in considerable detail a range of medical defects in a startlingly large number of children. In their first report for the years 1909–10 they had stated that their preliminary investigations clearly demonstrated the necessity of a service such as theirs, since they had shown 'the presence of an amount of physical defect which, were it not paralleled in other lands, would, by its magnitude, seem incredible . . . . This large amount of hitherto unsuspected defect in our midst has clearly demonstrated the necessity of our possessing an agency for its detection.'[48] The Victorian government were alarmed enough by these findings to provide Frank Tate, the Director of Education, with £169,000 in 1910 for new buildings or renovations in accordance with the advice of the medical officers and other public health officials.[49]

Others were less easily convinced. There was a feeling among some sections of the medical profession that the recording of relatively minor defects in children was unnecessary and possibly politically motivated. In 1916, the *Medical Journal of Australia* suggested there was an 'almost irresistible temptation' for a department of state government such as a school medical service, created for the sole purpose of finding defects, to boost its figures.[50] Certainly it was the case that some parents' reluctance to consult a doctor for their children on advice from the school medical officer was due to the fact that they considered the problem to be so trivial that they could treat it themselves. The British Medical Association of Australia (BMA) saw in this considerable cause for concern, since the public's perception of the necessity of proper medical treatment was, in their view, in danger of being eroded by what they characterized as irresponsible conduct on the part of the school medical officers.

Initially, the BMA gave its qualified approval to school medical inspection, the editor of the *Medical Journal of Australia* commenting in July 1914 that 'those who are concerned with the health of nations recognise that the care of the infant and of the school child is the first factor in the building up of a strong race'.[51] Nevertheless, there existed uneasy relationships between the school medical services and the BMA, the latter fearing the insidious imposition of government-funded medical schemes leading to the eventual nationalization of medical services. School medical inspection, baby health clinics, the bush nursing scheme and a growth in the number of government nominees on Hospital Boards were all cited as proof of the government's movement toward nationalization.[52]

In 1914, the four school medical officers in Victoria, realizing the impossibility of visiting all Victorian schools, suggested to the Minister of Public Instruction that bush nurses should undertake superficial examinations of school children in order to identify defects and also visit schools once a month and forward regular reports to the Department. The Minister approved the proposal and pledged to ask for £500 from the Legislative Council. However, a deputation to the Minister from the BMA expressed severe disapproval, arguing that bush nurses were fulfilling functions that should properly be undertaken by trained medical practitioners and that the preferable solution would be to appoint more medical officers.[53] Despite this representation from the BMA, the bush nursing scheme went ahead.[54]

Within eighteen months of this development, the fears of the BMA were brought into sharp relief in a dispute between the New South Wales Department of Public Instruction and the New South Wales Branch of the BMA. The furore broke out when the New South Wales Labour government announced its intention to establish a service of salaried medical practitioners to provide treatment for all school children, shown by inspection to have defects, regardless of parental income. The New South Wales government's scheme included the appointment of twenty full-time medical officers, seven full-time dentists, six part-time dentists, and a number of nurses, dental assistants and clerks.[55]

The New South Wales branch of the BMA had been at pains to stress that under no circumstances should the work of school medical inspection be combined with that of treatment. In accord with the procedures in other states, they believed that if a child was found to need treatment, parents should be sent a report and asked to consult their family doctor. If parents could not afford treatment, and did not belong to a Friendly Society that could provide assistance, then and only then should they be authorized to obtain treatment from a practitioner paid by the state. The fact that the Department of Public Instruction was planning to provide free medical treatment to all school children was viewed with horror by the BMA, as leading potentially to the nationalization of the whole medical profession.

Understandably, the public found it difficult to see the BMA's point of view and the medical profession was widely accused of self-interest, greed and callousness. In response to the public outcry, the editorial in a February 1916 issue of the *Medical Journal of Australia* was titled 'Misrepresentation'. One member stated 'we have been accused by the Minister of inhumanity and cruelty to the children and a sordid grasping after fees and the scandalous, though ridiculous, insinuation has been made that we do not want the school children treated because it would do away with their providing us with lots of work when they grow older'.[56] Mr Griffiths, the Minister of Education, invited representatives of the BMA to meet the other parties in the dispute and when they refused he threatened to introduce a Bill to compel them to meet under penalty of having their registration cancelled.

The dispute remained a subject of public and professional debate well into the following year. In May 1916, the New South Wales Minister for Education, Mr Griffiths, obtained unanimous support from the Political Labour League for the state government's policy of free medical treatment of school children.[57] The Chief Medical Officer in his official report on the New South Wales School Medical Service published in early 1917 also focused on the issue. He included statistics demonstrating that, in the absence of school clinics, only a small proportion of children obtained suitable treatment and stated his opinion that 'it is a waste of money to employ medical officers to examine school children if this examination does not result in treatment being obtained in a large proportion of those found to be physically defective'.[58]

However, it was not until July 1917 that an arrangement was made between the government and three metropolitan hospitals for the free treatment of school children.[59] Predictably, this led to a fresh outcry from the BMA. But the new Minister for Education, Mr James, had obviously lost patience with attempts to negotiate with the BMA and was not prepared to delay the scheme any longer. Speaking at a Health Conference on 25 July 1917, he was reported to have said that 'with reference to the question of the free treatment of children whose parents could afford to pay, he could make no difference in the schools. If it became a question of pauperizing certain scholars and losing the assistance of the British Medical Association, he was afraid he would lose the services of the Association.'[60]

Despite Mr James's resolution, the Department of Public Instruction in New South Wales was forced to limit its original scheme which proposed a dramatic expansion in the numbers of medical practitioners employed by the school medical service. Children in the metropolitan area were able to receive free treatment at one of the three metropolitan hospitals, but school children in country areas still had to wait for the travelling dental clinic, travelling ophthalmic clinic or travelling hospital to reach their district before free treatment was available. By 1920, it seems that there was a reversion to the procedure of examination only practised by the other states.[61]

School Medical Inspection and the Demise of Positive Eugenics

The period between 1909 to 1915 was the high point of eugenic influences on the work of the school medical service in Victoria. With the onset of the First World War, the number of staff was cut to half, though during the next five years Greig and Fitzgerald continued the service as usual but on a reduced scale. However, the early optimism of supporters of the notion that intervention and control of a benign Australian environment could generate a productive and efficient white race in the Antipodes waned considerably after the war, giving way to less positive solutions to the problem of racial weakness.[62] School anthropometrics had become a dead issue in the AAAS by the early 1920s. With the decline of this optimistic interventionist view and in the face of widespread criticism from the BMA and non-compliance from parents, the assuredness the medical officers had displayed before the war seemed increasingly difficult to sustain. Not only had the hereditary determinism of negative eugenics come to replace the environmentalism and optimism of positive eugenics as the orthodoxy among Australian eugenicists, but the limitation of the medical officers' role to inspection without subsequent treatment was a source of continuing frustration to them.

This is not to say that the medical service did not continue to receive support in some quarters for its work. In 1919, the editor of the *Medical Journal of Australia* commented that 'if the government of Victoria made an effort to meet its obligations to the young citizens of the State, twenty six additional medical officers would immediately be appointed'.[63] In October 1919 the editor purported to be scandalized when the Minister of Public Instruction devoted not a word to the mention of school hygiene or medical inspection in his annual report. He claimed that people might talk of wartime economies but it was 'actual extravagance to neglect the health of children at a time when the world needs efficiency to make good the waste of the war. Efficiency is impossible without health.'[64]

It was a recurring theme of the medical officers' own reports that their small numbers could not realize the ambitious goals they had set for themselves on the establishment of the service. The time the school medical officers were able to devote to school inspection after the war was limited by their other duties, including the preparation and delivery of lectures on hygiene at the Teachers' College, the Domestic Arts Hostel and the Swimming Schools, running special courses on the care of children, home nursing and first aid and the examination of candidates for the public service, of applicants for sick leave and of the women students at the Teachers' College.

Nevertheless, despite an increasingly desperate economic situation through the 1920s, the staff added to the Victorian service between 1920 and 1927 managed to avoid retrenchment, though no further appointments were made after 1927.[65] By 1928, the school medical service in Victoria consisted of eight medical officers (five women and three men), five part-time medical officers, eight dentists, nine dental assistants, two school nurses and two school disinfectors.[66] Distance and lack of funding conspired to restrict the service to metropolitan and major provincial centres until 1926, when local school committees began to pay travel costs for medical and dental officers. Jane Greig's proud claim as Chief Medical Inspector was that by 1930, school medical officers 'had visited every country district and every outpost in the State'.

A retrospective written by Greig in 1934 on the occasion of the twenty-fifth anniversary of the service reads, as perhaps might have been anticipated, as confirming the worth of the work of the school medical and dental staff. It was certainly more of a celebration of systematic and steady progress, albeit a cautious one, than a reflective exploration of the broader social and ethical issues which appeared so prominently in their early annual reports between 1909–15. Perhaps after 25 years Greig felt these matters went without saying. Or perhaps an account of increasing numbers of staff, increasing coverage of schools in the State of Victoria and the effective detection of defects were sufficient demonstration in themselves of the worth and continuing relevance of the service. Despite her concern for practical achievements, Greig's account might be described as a cautious celebration only because the service's expansionist plans to be able to examine every child in Victorian schools at regular intervals were only partly achieved.[67]

The struggle to continue to expand medical inspection to a level deemed satisfactory by the service's staff may explain why there is little attention given to eugenics-related matters by 1935 compared to the early reports. At the same time, the school medical officers had continued to elicit information on the racial origins of children's parents and grandparents throughout the 1920s and into the 1930s, though parents continued to be suspicious of why it was necessary to divulge such information and of how it might be used.[68] Moreover, there is some evidence to suggest that Greig's concern for practicalities were not entirely divorced from other, less material considerations. There had certainly been continuity within the service in terms of staffing, since Greig herself had been with the medical service from its inception, and on her retirement in 1937 Eileen Fitzgerald, who joined the staff in 1913, became her successor as Chief Medical Inspector.

Summing up the service's achievements near the end of her retrospective, Greig remarked that 'we knew the defects of the children and we knew the requirements to remedy these; and we felt that, in a short time, we should be able to keep the Australian child free from physical defects and give it a chance of being what it has always given promise of being – the best in the world'.[69] In another paper published in the *Medical Journal of Australia* in February 1934, Greig argued in a similar vein that Australian children's freedom from serious defects combined with the fact that they were heavier and taller than the average English child, gave Australia a chance to produce a stalwart race if only the minor defects still existing could be remedied. The aim of preventative medicine, according to Greig, should be to produce a healthy people with a constant efficiency and endurance which could use its special abilities to the utmost.[70]

But these lingering influences of a positive, environmental view of eugenics were superseded by the emergence of the Mental Hygiene movement in the late 1920s and 1930s. This movement spawned organizations such as the Racial Hygiene Association and the Institute of Family Relations. The latter promoted sex education, pre-marital examinations and birth control for eugenic purposes, on the basis of the view that improvement of the race depended upon limiting the offspring of unhealthy or unsuitable couples.[71] The more extreme sections of this movement advocated both voluntary and compulsory sterilization of the feeble-minded and other defectives.[72] As forms of negative eugenics began to receive renewed support in Australia and elsewhere, there had been little or no attempt on the part of Greig or her colleagues to reconceptualize their mission. The justifications they gave for the work of the school medical services, on the rare occasion they were articulated, seemed to have changed little from the initial rationale developed during their first five years. The growing influence of hereditary determinism in Australia provided little rhetorical support for a service which claimed to be able to resolve a range of problems associated with progeniture and breeding through medical and educational intervention.

Mirroring similar moves in Britain, the relationship between the school medical service and the Education Department ended in Victoria in October 1943 when control of the service passed to the Department of Health in accordance with the provisions of the new Health Act of that year. The possibility of such an arrangement had been entertained from time to time since before the medical service was established, though until the late 1930s, the administration of medical inspection in schools seemed to be more easily accomplished through the offices of the Department of Education.[73] By 1943, and in addition to the routine work of medical inspection, the school medical service engaged in a range of special surveys of vision defects, child labour in rural areas, children in Housing Commission settlements and nutrition.[74] These topics present quite a different agenda to that which framed the mission of the school medical service in Victoria on its establishment in 1909.

Resisting Bodies

It may be accurate to speak of the demise of militarized physical training, though it could be argued that school medical inspection was able to survive through the interwar years and re-invent itself to better fit new times and new forms of public discourse in the 1940s. At the same time, as this and the previous chapters have aimed to show, the militarist and eugenicist agendas in which physical training and medical inspection were embedded contributed to the project of schooling bodies through their obsessive attention to detailed working on bodies, their examination, measurement and categorization, and their training in the use of space and time through specific and precise movements.

The highly codified forms of medical inspection and physical training that appeared in Australian schools towards the end of the first decade of this century can be viewed as late and sophisticated products of disciplinary society. These disciplinary technologies were ill suited to schooling bodies following the First World War when public discourse changed dramatically. Both sets of practices continued to operate into the 1930s and 1940s, but they belonged to another era in which drilling and examining children's bodies seemed necessary and appropriate to social order, racial regeneration, defence, national identity and economic productivity. While attempting to school bodies, physical training and medical inspection seemed increasingly instead to produce resisting bodies, bodies that were constructed within different forms of public discourse, and that made sense on different terms.

Anti-war sentiments, new metaphors for national identity, limited public spending linked to economic depression, the rise of negative eugenics and right-wing politics;[75] each of these shifts in public discourse contributed to the logic of the resisting body in the face of militarized physical training and eugenics-inspired medical inspection. We are forced to recognize these real limitations on the effectiveness of these technologies of biopower in schooling bodies. But it would be incorrect to assume that these school practices had no success in normalizing and regulating children's bodies.

There can be no doubt that, if followed to the letter, the Swedish system of physical training embodied a formal and militaristic pedagogy, despite its remedial and therapeutic uses. Teachers were required to teach according to a script, memorizing the fixed sequence of activities and their progressions, and these prescriptions were then mapped on to the bodies of the children as they performed the movements that the system demanded. It was the requirement for absolute correctness of performance that lay at the heart of physical training's contribution to schooling bodies, and it was this requirement for perfection that undermined its effectiveness. The Swedish system was a complex and intricate one to master, as Bjelke-Petersen on more than one occasion pointed out,[76] and taught badly it was most likely to produce resisting rather than schooled bodies. But not all children suffered drilling and exercising as tedious and meaningless movement, and many actually enjoyed it, particularly when it was well taught.

The encoding of normality within the practices of medical inspection, embedded as these were within the ideals of positive eugenics, were indisputably powerful means of positioning particular individuals and groups in Australian society as in some respects 'physically defective' and, by imputation, morally deficient. People thus positioned by this discourse clearly could play little or no part in forging a robust white race in the southern hemisphere, and their exclusion from significant participation in decision making which affected their lives could be legitimated by reference to a scientifically derived definition of the 'normal Australian'. Within this discourse, Aboriginals were denied any possibility of being acknowledged as Australians since their bodies were perceived to be too exotically different from the idealized norm of the Anglo-Celt.

Moreover, in the absence of personal and specific oral testimony, we can only guess at the effects on children of being classified as in some way physically 'defective'.[77] But it is at this level of children's consciousness of their bodies, particularly during the formative years of subjective self-awareness, that the normative and regulative imperatives of school medical inspection were most likely to manifest themselves. For a number of generations of Australians, physical imperfection was a medically and scientifically legitimated fact of life, confirming prejudices against all forms of unconventionality in appearance and behaviour as 'abnormal' and, by implication, unAustralian. Only the resistance of parents to the monopolizing activities of the medical profession as a whole would seem to have offered some means of counteracting the establishment of medicalized definitions of normality. On the other hand, the encoding of physical defects as abnormal within medical discourse may merely have confirmed, and perhaps extended, already existing prejudices among the population.

While the effects of school anthropometry and medical inspection may be somewhat difficult to discern in terms of their impact on social regulation and normalization, there are fairly clear-cut temporal boundaries surrounding their practice. The growing influence of hereditary determinism between the wars offered little support to the view that detailed knowledge of children's bodies could form the basis of medical and militaristic interventions which would improve the quality of the Anglo-Celtic race in Australia, and effectively disqualified the regulatory and normative strategies which lay at the heart of this rationale. The 'heavy, ponderous, meticulous and constant' attention to the body which Foucault[78] identified as characteristic of such institutions as prisons, the military and schools throughout the nineteenth century seems by the 1920s and 1930s to have been relaxed or, at least, applied less systematically and vigorously.

In school physical training, the formalism of physical and military drill began to give way to comparatively liberalized forms of movement including rhythmic activities for younger children and girls and games and sports for boys and girls. But this does not mean that the body had necessarily become any less important strategically as a site of regulation and normalization. On the contrary, the intensifying interest in 'building the body beautiful'[79] along with mass participation in sports and games through the 1930s and 1940s signalled the beginnings of a shift in the forms of corporeal regulation rather than a lack of interest in or neglect of the body. It is to these alternative, 'looser' forms of schooling bodies that we turn in the next chapter.

Notes and References

1 Donald Macdonald in the *Argus*, 7 April 1917.
2 Dr Antill Pockley in the *Medical Journal of Australia*, 12 February 1916, pp. 142–3.
3 Minister of Public Instruction (1912) *Education Report for the Year 1911–12* Melbourne: Government Printer, p. 29.
4 *Argus*, 8 October 1912.
5 Donald Macdonald in the *Argus*, 10 January 1912.
6 Australian Archives Victoria (AAV), MP 84-1, 1832/13/585, Conference Report, 1912.
7 AAV, MP 84-1, 1832/13/573, letter 26 September 1912.
8 *Argus*, 10 May 1913, p. 16.
9 Minister of Public Instruction (1916) *Education Report for the Year 1915–1916* Melbourne: Government Printer, p. 11.
10 *Argus*, 10 May 1913, p. 16.
11 Cf. Kirk, D. (1992) *Defining Physical Education: The Social Construction of a School Subject in Postwar Britain* London: Falmer, Chapter 4.
12 AAV, MP 84-1, 1832/13/573, 27 August 1912, internal minute paper to Adjutant General.
13 *Argus*, 14 May 1913.

14 *Argus*, 17 March 1913, p. 12.

15 *Argus*, 14 May 1913.

16 Jauncey claims junior cadets only had to be registered, see Jauncey, L.C. (1935) *The Story of Conscription in Australia* London: Allen & Unwin, p. 36. The cadets were nevertheless liable to prosecution under section 135 of the Act (see Fletcher, J.P. and Hills, J.F. (1919) *Conscription Under Camouflage: An Account of Compulsory Military Training in Australasia Down to the Outbreak of the Great War* Adelaide, pp. 13–14). It is not clear whether or how many junior cadets were actually prosecuted, however. Tanner's comments suggest that they were, pointing to amendments to section 135 of the Act which reduced the maximum fine from £100 to £5, thereby rendering prosecution less severe. Moreover, the amendments stipulated that those under 16 had to be tried in a children's court and those who could not pay the fine should not be sent to jail but submitted to the custody of 'any prescribed authority', Tanner, T.W. (1980) *Compulsory Citizen Soldiers* Waterloo, NSW: Alternative Publishing Cooperative, p. 204.

17 In Hurley, F.T. (1972) Compulsory military training and the conscription referendum 1911–1916. Unpublished MA Thesis, University of Melbourne, pp. 23-6.

18 *Argus*, 14 May 1913.

19 Crawford, R. (1981) A history of physical education in Victoria and New South Wales 1872–1939: with particular reference to English precedent. Unpublished PhD Thesis, La Trobe University, p. 338.

20 *Argus*, 5 May 1913.

21 We can counterpoise these reactions with Hurley's claim that there was general ambivalence towards and acceptance of the scheme through the first two years 1911–13, see Hurley, Compulsory military training, pp. 28–9; and Barrett's that it was generally accepted, Barrett, J. (1979) *Falling In: Australians and 'Boy Conscription' 1911–15* Sydney: Hale & Iremonger, p. 132.

22 Tanner, *Compulsory Citizen Soldiers*, p. 204.

23 Minister of Public Instruction (1915) *Education Report for the Year 1914–1915* Melbourne: Government Printer, p. 28.

24 Donald Macdonald in the *Argus*, 7 April 1917.

25 Searle, G. (1965) The digger tradition and Australian nationalism *Meanjin Quarterly*, **24** (2), pp. 152–4.

26 Tanner has made a similar observation, Tanner, *Compulsory Citizen Soldiers*, p. 228.

27 AAV, MP 367, 629/22/97, Reports on Physical Training 1918–1920, Interim Report of Inspections made in the Second Military District, December 1919.

28 An example can be found in the Victorian Education Department's *Education Gazette and Teachers' Aid*, January 1919.

29 Virtue, R. (1922) Physical training for children of the infants' school, Victorian Education Department's *Education Gazette and Teachers' Aid*, January.

30 Crawford, R. (1979) The educational renaissance in Australian schools, 1901–1931: the strange case of physical education, in the *Proceedings of the Fourth Canadian Symposium on the History of Sport and Physical Education* Vancouver, pp. 1–20.

31 The Defence Department initially employed a staff of 18 in 1911; by 1931 this had been reduced to 8, running at the total cost of £4000 per annum, AAV, MP 84-1, 929/17/25.

32 *Argus*, 1 November 1929.
33 *Argus*, 2 November 1929, p. 18.
34 *Sydney Herald*, 16 May 1931; *Age*, 20 May 1931.
35 *Argus*, 11 November 1929.
36 *Argus*, 2 November 1929, p. 19.
37 AAV, MP 84-1, 929/17/25, 22 August 1930.
38 Minister of Public Instruction (1929) *Education Report for the Year 1928–29* Melbourne: Government Printer.
39 AAV, MP 84-1, 929/17/25, 4 September 1930, letter to the Premier of NSW from the NSW Director of Education; Minister of Public Instruction (1931) *Education Report for the Year 1930–1* Melbourne: Government Printer, p. 6.
40 *Argus*, 22 July 1911, p. 7.
41 *Medical Journal of Australia*, 30 April 1921, p. 362.
42 *Argus*, 24 February 1915, p. 13.
43 *Medical Journal of Australia*, 6 March 1915, p. 216.
44 Walker, D. (1987) Mind and body, in Gammage, B. and Spearritt, P. (eds) *Australians 1938* Broadway: Fairfax, Syme and Weldon Associates, pp. 232–3.
45 *Argus*, 12 August 1911.
46 *Argus*, 16 February 1910.
47 *Argus*, 31 December 1930, p. 13.
48 *Medical Journal of Australia*, 12 February 1916, p. 142.
49 Anchen, J.C. (1956) *Frank Tate and His Work for Education* Melbourne: ACER.
50 *Medical Journal of Australia*, 12 February 1916, pp. 142–3.
51 *Medical Journal of Australia*, 25 July 1914.
52 *Medical Journal of Australia*, 22 January 1916, p. 82.
53 *Medical Journal of Australia*, 8 August 1914, p. 144.
54 Minister of Public Instruction (1915) *Education Report for the Year 1914–1915* Melbourne: Government Printer, pp. 27–8.
55 *Medical Journal of Australia*, 21 July 1917.
56 *Medical Journal of Australia*, 12 February 1916, p. 143.
57 *Medical Journal of Australia*, 13 May 1916, p. 399.
58 *Medical Journal of Australia*, 21 July 1917, p. 59.
59 *Medical Journal of Australia*, 21 July 1917, p. 63.
60 *Medical Journal of Australia*, 4 August 1917, p. 111.
61 As the *Medical Journal of Australia* notes, in New South Wales 'the child discovered to be suffering from a defect (i)s required to be treated by its own medical attendant' (*MJA*, 18 September 1920, p. 301).
62 Bacchi, C. (1980) The nature–nurture debate in Australia, 1900–1914 *Historical Studies* **19** (5), p. 211.
63 *Medical Journal of Australia*, 25 January 1919, p. 76.
64 *Medical Journal of Australia*, 18 October 1919, p. 344.
65 This matter continued to be a bone of contention in the late 1930s – see Fitzgerald's report as Chief Medical Inspector in Minister of Public Instruction (1939) *Education Report for the Year 1938–1939* Melbourne: Government Printer, p. 37.
66 Minister of Public Instruction (1929) *Education Report for the Year 1928–1929* Melbourne: Government Printer, p. 9.
67 Minister of Public Instruction (1935) *Education Report for the Year 1934–1935* Melbourne: Government Printer, p. 24.

68 *Argus*, 31 December 1930, p. 13.
69 Minister of Public Instruction Report, 1934–1935, p. 24.
70 *Medical Journal of Australia*, 17 February 1934, p. 240.
71 Curthoys, A. (1989) Eugenics, feminism and birth control: the case of Marion Diddington *Hecate*, 14–15, p. 80.
72 Booth, A. (1934) Negative Eugenics: how shall we deal with feeblemindedness? *Argus*, 12 January, p. 6; *Australian Racial Hygiene Congress Report*, 15–18 September 1929.
73 *Medical Journal of Australia*, 30 April 1921; and 20 November 1926.
74 Waddington, D.M., Radford, W.C. and Keats, J.A. (eds) (1948) *Review of Education in Australia 1940–1948* ACER: Melbourne University Press, p. 65.
75 Macintyre, S. (1993) *The Oxford History of Australia (Volume 4) 1901–1942* Melbourne: Oxford University Press.
76 AAV, MP 84-1, 1832/13/573, 17 June 1912, internal minute paper to Adjutant General.
77 Francis, R.I. (1979) Schools from the pupils' point of view. New South Wales in the late colonial period *Journal of the Australian and New Zealand History of Education Society*, **8** (2) 2, pp. 22–35.
78 Foucault, M. (1980) *Power/Knowledge: Selected Interviews and Other Writings* Brighton: Harvester Press (Trans. C. Gordon).
79 Matthews, J.J. (1987) Building the body beautiful *Australian Feminist Studies*, **5**, Summer, pp. 17–34.

5

Civilizing Bodies: The Games Ethic and Sport in Schools

The development of well-supervised sport among the boys and girls attending our high schools is important, and should show effect at no distant date; for sport has come to stay in the schools. Our boys and girls will go forth physically better equipped and socially more adaptable than in the past, and should take with them ideals that will gradually place sport in the State on a very high level, and it is not unreasonable to hope that they will so influence sporting public opinion that little of the undesirable will be left in popular contests and displays.[1]

The rise of sport in mass schooling signals an important shift in the technologies of power employed to school bodies, from the meticulous and ponderous to looser forms of power over the body. This shift did not happen abruptly, but instead spun out over a period of at least 70 years, between the last few decades of the nineteenth century to the middle of the twentieth, from its origins in the pastimes of the sons and daughters of the privileged classes to its emerging prominence in schools for the masses by the end of the Second World War. While the competitive team games that made up the bulk of sport in schools marked a sharp contrast to the regimentation of drilling and exercising, they nevertheless need to be viewed as a technology of power and a means of regulating bodies in space and time. More than this, the team games originating in the practices of the privileged classes were viewed as a means of civilizing the bodies of the children of the working classes.

Team games are paradigm cases of disciplinary technology. The game can only exist if participants agree to abide by a set of arbitrary rules that define the purpose of the game and the space that constitutes the playing area. These rules also govern where participants can move within that area, often restricting movement according to the player's position and function in a team, and how participants should move, through the formalization of techniques, skills and strategies. The design of equipment, playing surfaces and other technological developments further prescribe how bodies might move, and the kind of bodies that might participate in games. And team games require particular forms of social relations between players on the same side and on opposing sides. In light of these techniques for regulating bodies, it is not surprising that social commentators and educators found in team games a rich source of prescriptions for human conduct beyond the games themselves.

The team games that gained prominence in school practices by the middle of this century showed little of the meticulous and precise attention to detailed drilling and examining of children's bodies that characterized physical training and school medical inspection. Just the same, they belonged to the same family of practices concerned with schooling children's bodies. They did this by attempting to produce civilized bodies, at first embedded in the public discourses informing the ways of life of the socially privileged classes of Australia and Britain, but gradually resonating with new forms of public discourse that were shaping the practices of wider society following the First World War. While they were embedded in new discourses, they also presented opportunities to conserve and consolidate particular orders of society, especially the gender order, since the ways of playing games were strictly differentiated by femaleness and maleness.[2]

The growing prominence of sport in government schools during the 1920s and 1930s, and the widespread conviction of educators, politicians and social commentators that games offered an unrivalled educational medium for the development of civilizing values, signalled the coming of a new mass regime of the body. But as Michel Foucault guessed, the shift to this looser form of power over the body in the rise to prominence of games and of attempts to produce civilized bodies did not constitute a break with modernity. The mass school as an institution continued to require the regulation of children's bodies in order to pursue its social and educational missions.

Following the devastation of world war, economic depression and in the foreshadows of fascism and the concentration camps, mass drilling and medical inspection held new and sinister connotations. But since bodies continued to 'matter' schooling, alternative forms of corporeal regulation began to be employed. Sport in the form of team games seemed to present a more acceptable alternative to schooling bodies than physical training and medical inspection. This chapter traces the rise to prominence of competitive team games in school practices and the production of civilized bodies connoting social cohesion, controlled aggression and appropriately gendered behaviour.

The Emergence and Dissemination of the English Public School Games Ethic

In Australia, competitive team games and the English public school games ethic had a profound impact on the conduct of sport in both private and government schools between the beginning of the twentieth century and the end of the Second World War. This influence arrived in the government schools primarily through the voluntary organization of games as an extra-curricular pursuit following their development in the schools serving Australia's social elites, eventually to occupy a place in the regular school curriculum in the form of physical education.

In *The Games Ethic and Imperialism*, J.A. Mangan argued that the diffusion of English public school ball games, particularly cricket and football, and the inculcation of Christian manliness, was a key strategy by which the British Empire was sustained. Mangan has shown that integral to the notion of manliness, which lay at the heart of the games ethic, was leadership and the moral imperative of the British gentleman to command. A later development of the notion of manliness added to dominance the dimension of deference, where it was believed that the games ethic's 'inculcation promoted not simply initiative and self-reliance but also loyalty and obedience'.[3] According to Mangan, this dual purpose was well suited to the tasks of colonialism and social class demarcation, since it permitted emulation of and deference to social superiors while at the same time facilitating dominance over and distancing from perceived inferiors.

The moral imperative that drove the process of colonialism sought to teach respect and deference for a particular version of British culture, while fostering in schoolboys in the various far-flung corners of the globe a sense of their own right to lead. The process was colonialist and imperialist in so far as the instincts nurtured in this future leadership class in each part of the Empire, regardless of local culture, were British. At the same time, local culture could not be easily denied, and Mangan points out with reference to the specific cases of the Sudan, tropical Africa, India and Canada, that the games ethic was reconstructed in each of these settings. In Canada, for instance, Mangan showed that the games ethic served complex and somewhat contradictory purposes, providing a means of loyalist identification with Britain and the British crown, but also feeding a separate Canadian national identity, while its key tenets were perceived to be threatened by American influences. 'The outcome', remarks Mangan, 'was integration, compromise and adjustment.'[4]

Similarly complex processes can be seen at work in relation to social class. Mangan argued that the English grammar schools of the Victorian and Edwardian eras evolved with concerns for social status and prestige uppermost, and that they modelled themselves on their perceived social superiors, the public schools. They also sought simultaneously to distance themselves from their perceived social inferiors, and competitive team games played a key role in this process. Games provided schools with a highly visible and dynamic medium in which to display the values associated with manliness. Possession of the material resources required to play games, such as playing fields and other facilities, were prominent symbols of social superiority.

> Playing fields were part of the social and cultural capital to be acquired in the struggle to maintain social position. In this process they served as a means of demonstrating image. They were at one and the same time emblems of similarity and separateness. But above all they were symbols of superiority – not merely social but moral. Schools without them were suspect. They were either inferior institutions of narrow vocationalism or anachronistic institutions of dangerous intellectualism.[5]

This use of the playing field as a highly visible symbol of social superiority, and the use of games playing in processes of social deference, domination, emulation and distancing, were predicated on the hierarchical nature of British society during the Victorian and Edwardian eras. These processes reveal something of the transitory nature of this hierarchy since games playing and the schools themselves were a necessary means of obtaining the moral and other cultural credentials for moving up the social ladder. From this perspective, the spilling of the games ethic and games playing over into the schools at the lower levels of the British bourgeois classes can be seen as an extension of the original purpose of the games ethic in the public schools. The consolidation of this ethic in the grammar schools, many achieving the status of 'Public School' during the late Victorian and Edwardian period, did much to cherish and perpetuate its key values in a living form within the upper strata of the British bourgeoisie.[6]

Dominance and deference, social emulation and distancing: these are key tensions identified by Mangan in his account of the dissemination of the games ethic beyond temporal and spatial boundaries and across the social hierarchies of the middle classes. These complex and somewhat contradictory processes provide a useful framework within which to view the social consequences of the transplantation of competitive team games and the games ethic in Australian government schools, since it allows us to consider how Australian national identities and concomitant civilized bodies were constructed out of a British colonial and class-conscious heritage.

Civilizing Male Bodies: The Games Ethic in
Australia's Elite Schools

Geoffrey Sherington[7] has shown how the English public school games ethic
was transplanted in Australian society through the efforts of former pupils
of England's elite schools for boys and former students of her ancient
universities who became members of staff of Australia's elite schools.
Sherington emphasized the role of the Athletic Association of the Great
Public Schools (AAGPS) in New South Wales in 1892 in the institution-
alization of the games ethic within the schools serving Australia's social
elites. The advent of this Association was the result of a decision by ten
private schools in and around Sydney to organize inter-school competitions
in cricket, rugby union, rowing and athletics. From the outset, the Association aimed to perform regulative and normative functions, standardizing
rules, specifying age gradings, and consolidating the value system in which
games playing was embedded.

The invention of the term 'great public school' to describe the Association's membership reveals the efforts the schools made to insulate themselves from other private institutions, self-consciously echoing the
terminology of the elite English schools, while sharply marking off any
association with government elementary ('public') schools. Entry of new
schools was rigorously policed by the AAGPS. The only new members to
be admitted before 1900 were the Armidale School and the Scots College,
and after several unsuccessful attempts, the state-sponsored Sydney High
School in 1906. Thereafter, the Association refused membership to other
applicants, effectively establishing its members as the most exclusive (and
exclusionary) private schools for boys in New South Wales. The Association
also refused to add other sports to the original four, conceding only to rifle
shooting in 1905 and some limited sponsorship of swimming competitions
in 1909.

As Sherington points out, the delimitation of games and sports officially
sanctioned by the AAGPS was a clear case of social editing. By acting as it
did, the Association was able to attribute to these activities an elite status,
deeply embedded in the amateur ideal, and to establish games as effective
educational instruments for a leadership class. More than this, 'membership
of the Association provided the necessary imprimatur of status. The
shortened prefix of "GPS" became synonymous with a school which drew
much of its status from participation in organized games competitions.'[8]
Such was the symbolic power of these amateur sports activities among the
middle classes that membership of an athletic association was the means of
demarcating social status. The importance of the exclusiveness of AAGPS
membership became even greater when other private institutions and

state-sponsored high schools were able to compete on a relatively equal footing with the GPS schools in public examinations.

A similar situation was unfolding in Victoria. The first recorded football match in Victoria of any kind was between Scotch College and Melbourne Grammar School on 7 August 1858.[9] A cricket match had taken place earlier that year, in February, between Scotch and Geelong Grammar School. From 1885, football and cricket matches were organized on a regular basis between private schools in the Melbourne area and, in 1891, six schools for boys organized themselves as the Associated Public Schools, with the intention of regulating the conduct of sporting fixtures.

Ray Crawford[10] illustrated how a version of the games ethic was promoted in the upper echelons of Victorian society through a study of the work of L.A. Adamson at Wesley College in Melbourne. As Headmaster of Wesley for thirty years between 1902 and 1932, Adamson was to become a key figure in promoting Christian manliness as a system of values for training boys to become gentlemen within a leadership class. He also considered that the values constituting the games ethic could, in a more general way, underpin the entire social order in Australia. His occupancy of a number of key positions within a range of upper-class institutions, such as membership of the Board of the Faculty of Arts and the Council of the University of Melbourne, of the School Board which controlled public examinations, and his participation in the second Melbourne Conference on Physical Training in 1910, made Adamson a highly visible and influential figure within opinion-making circles in Melbourne.

Under Adamson, Wesley instituted a whole range of activities, such as school assemblies, a school magazine, sports colours, military cadet training, school songs, banquets for victorious sports teams, and speech days that were aimed at the development of a school ethos feeding into the process of creating Christian gentlemen. Games were only one element in this matrix of interlinking practices, but a vitally important one, since they were a dynamic medium for the promulgation of Adamson's educational doctrine of 'strenuousness and sentiment', which expressed all of the key features of Anglo-Celtic manliness.

Through the activities of the APS in Victoria, the AAGPS in New South Wales, and similar associations developing in the other states by 1911,[11] the place of competitive team games and the values and beliefs constituting a version of the games ethic had been firmly established within the private school system by the beginning of the twentieth century. These associations worked very effectively as a means of disallowing contact with schools considered to be serving less elite members of the community. In similar fashion to the process unfolding in Edwardian Britain, schools serving the lower ranks of the middle classes began to utilize games to emulate their social superiors and distance themselves from lesser private schools.[12] In

Victoria, and after at least one relatively unsuccessful attempt in the 1890s, eight boys' grammar schools followed the six public schools' example and in 1921 formed themselves into the Associated Grammar Schools, carrying on regular premiership contests in cricket, football, athletics, swimming and tennis, and thereby consolidating their place in the social hierarchy.

Between 1900 and 1914, the games playing of Australia's male social elites became increasingly visible to the general public. The public schools' sport contests received regular and detailed attention in the press.[13] In this respect, the sporting activities of the public schools captured the public's interest, but not as symbolic forms of leadership education. Interest was in the outcome of the contest itself. Even among the schools, in the few years leading up to the First World War, there were already signs that the lust for the contest was overriding respect for some of the higher values that the practice of games was intended to develop through the process of civilizing bodies. While the games ethic was continually reinforced as a system of values, and eagerly repeated on speech nights, the practice of games playing was underpinned increasingly by a different set of assumptions.

Reports in the daily press of sports contests between elite schools for boys became commonplace in the years approaching the beginning of the First World War. The stakes for the schools concerned were high. Winning the premiership in football, cricket and the Head of the River boat race gave the successful school tremendous prominence in the communities it served. For these reasons, and for all the expressions of higher values by head-masters, there can be little doubt that by the early 1900s competitive team games had gathered a cult following in which excessive behaviour was indulged. As Greg Dening suggests, in his centenary portrait of Xavier College in Melbourne, there was little of the higher ideals of the games ethic in evidence when it came to the business of keeping score.

> School sport at the time Xavier entered it (c.1898) was highly aggressive and competitive. It became more so in the second and third decades of the twentieth century. There is plenty of evidence to suggest that playing the game was not nearly as important as winning. For Xavier, the ten years before their championship wins in football and cricket in 1910 were bleak and humiliating. 1907 was remembered as a particularly humbling season in which Scotch, with some scorn for Xavier's pride, played not so much to win as to give their full-forward a goal-kicking record. He kicked 21 goals 12 behinds out of a score of 24 goals 20 behinds. That gave some piquancy to Xavier's defeat of Scotch for the championship in 1910. It also gave some vigour to their meetings for years after. When a Xavier boy removed a tooth from a Scotch boy in 1916 and the incident reached the papers, the Xavarian protested that bumps were given in a friendly spirit and that if two

Xavier boys were in hospital for a fortnight after a 'knee-stroke in the kidneys', it was still the 'pleasantest match of the season'. And in any case the Scotch captain visited Gorman in hospital! However, even the most pleasant matches for players upset supporters. There were scuffles and 'broo-has' between Scotch and Xavier boys in 1914, 1915, 1916 and in 1917 the general behaviour of the schoolboy crowds led to the suspension of premiership sport.[14]

Civilizing the bodies of privileged young men though games playing was intended to reinforce heterosexuality and a form of masculinity that accepted authority and order as natural, and valued controlled aggression and sanctioned forms of physical violence to maintain and reinforce this natural order. Indeed, there was a widespread view among headmasters of elite schools for boys in the second half of the nineteenth century that games playing was an antidote to homosexuality. A strict timetable of activities that completely occupied the working and leisure hours of boarding school boys sought to reduce the opportunities for their participation in 'immoral' behaviours and, when they were able to escape the suffocating confines of this regime, to render them too exhausted to be sexually active. This, in any case, was the pious hope of many head teachers, though there is substantial evidence in the memoirs and other writing of former public schoolboys to suggest that sexual relationships between boys were commonplace, despite the schools' imposition of games on all pupils. Ironically, it was the athlete, rather than the scholar, who became the prime object of sexual desire and potency within public schoolboy culture.[15]

In addition to the schools' use of games to subdue homosexual activity, there was a constant need for vigilance in case the higher values of civilizing the future leadership class might be corrupted by the desire to win at all costs. There was too much to be gained and lost in this process for schools to be ambivalent about the conduct of games and sport, and school head teachers and other agents of the games ethic waged a ceaseless battle on behalf of what they saw as the true spirit of games while indulging in the fruits of victory. Despite these tensions, as a system of values and a means of demarcating social status, they saw the games ethic as too valuable to be restricted to boys' schools alone, and in the 1890s games began to gain a foothold in schools for girls.

Civilizing Female Bodies

We need to note that women were not expected to adopt the leadership roles of their brothers, husbands and fathers, and so while games playing was promoted in the elite schools for girls, Crawford[16] suggests that it lacked the fervour that was developing in boys' schools. The differences in girls' schools clearly reflected the social roles middle-class women were expected to play, mainly as wife, mother, house-manager and home-maker. Moreover, games were not viewed within the schools for girls as a means of reinforcing heterosexuality as they were in the schools for boys. Nevertheless, the effects of games and the games ethic on these schools was profound. The most popular games were croquet, tennis and, later, hockey, initially organized by the girls themselves. It was only during the first decade of the twentieth century that school administrators began to see the benefits of a more organized approach to games in terms of generating a corporate identity for their schools, a matter that became all the more pressing when the new standards forced on all non-government schools by the Registration Act of 1908 laid them open to competition for pupils from the newly established government secondary schools.[17]

Inter-school competition began to be taken very seriously by some schools for girls, evidenced by the formation of organizations such as the Girls' Schools Hockey Association in 1905. The schools for girls, like those for boys, also began to eulogize the system of values surrounding games. To play games was to prepare for the Great Game of Life!

And so when you're playing the great game of life
And your days are all over at school
When you're faced with a problem that cannot be solved
By merely applying a rule:
There's an easy way out, but it's not quite so straight
Play the game, choose the clean one and meet with your fate – As a
    sport.[18]

As might have been expected, in tandem with this growing interest and increasing seriousness about games came expressions of concern in school magazines which warned of the dangers of 'winning at all costs'. The construction of an appropriate form of femininity was of primary importance in these schools, and so the question of boisterousness and unladylike behaviour was continually being addressed. This concern lead to the appearance of ambivalence towards competitive sport on occasion, and the schools themselves were keenly sensitive to charges of over-zealousness. At Tintern School, parents were reassured in the 1906 prospectus that the school realized the danger of 'girls becoming boisterous in games and are most particular that the behaviour at play is such as is becoming to ladies'.[19] The growing attractions of games did not supplant the other element of physical culture in these schools, and Dano-Swedish gymnastics in its purer, therapeutic and non-militaristic form had a significant influence in civilizing female bodies. Indeed, the position of gymnastics alongside games was safeguarded by the influence of several women employed by the private schools as teachers of physical culture who had trained either in one of the elite women's colleges in Britain, or in Australia trained privately by one of the leading physical culturists of the day.[20]

Nevertheless, while the same excesses of the cult of athleticism common in the boys' schools were not replicated in the girls' schools, games playing formed a substantial component in the education of socially privileged girls in a manner similar to their brothers. What was most important was the system of values that surrounded games playing in these schools, where it was widely held as an ideal, at least, if not always in practice, that 'sport develops the best in us. We have to sink personal feelings for the good of our side. We want to win – why? Not for personal glory but for the honour of our School. This idea of honour is a very high one and if we really learn what it is at school, we carry it with us through our lives.'[21]

Just as the civilizing of young men's bodies projected a form of hetero-sexual masculinity, so the civilizing of female bodies involved attempts to balance physical development and health in the cause of child bearing and rearing with appropriate ways of moving and being embodied that projected a form of femininity appropriate to privileged young women's place in the social order. The female body was civilized for service to her family and future husband, her children and her country.

Sport, Nationhood and Social Conflict in Australia

The diffusion of these versions of the games ethic through the elite private schools had, by the end of the first decade of the twentieth century, led to the wide acceptance by the Australian middle classes of the system of values surrounding competitive team games.[22] Moreover, these values were components of a world view. The values system in which the playing of team games was embedded crystallized proper social conduct and social order, exemplified duty and responsibility in civilized society, and located various groups and individuals, women and men, in their right and proper place within society. However, the codes of right conduct, social order, and loyalty to Britain and the monarchy that team games symbolized for the middle classes, and the contrasting world views of other Australians, was soon to be exposed by the coming crisis of the First World War.

According to Michael McKernan,[23] the First World War made visible a number of underlying tensions in Australian society that found expression in and around sport, particularly those tensions associated with social class and religion. The conflicts that surfaced during the war years show the extent to which some ideas about sport had gained wide currency within sections of Australian society in the thirty-year period prior to the war. The war prompted a public declaration of these ideas, and their explicit articulation, codification and legitimation to an extent that had not occurred prior to 1914.

McKernan argued that two distinct views of sport declared themselves near the beginning of the war, one held mainly by country Australians and the middle classes, and the other by the urban working classes. The former group championed an amateur ethic, in which sport 'had meaning in so far as it taught the young such values as loyalty, determination, unselfishness and the team spirit'.[24] The latter group propagated the professional view, in which 'sport meant entertainment and pleasure, an exciting break from the monotony of urban work'. McKernan suggested that during the war, tensions between these two groups became focused around the question of the priority that should be given to the defence of the Empire, and the two views of sport emerged as an important element in this conflict.

The middle-class opinion-makers who subscribed to the amateur view called for sport to be abandoned during wartime since, they claimed, it dissipated the nation's efforts and distracted the energies of healthy young men who otherwise could be occupied bearing arms. The administrators and other spokesmen for professional sport maintained that sport should continue because it provided some release from the hardships and horrors of the war. McKernan remarked that the ensuing debate generated great acrimony because the opposing camps were divided along class and religious lines.

For instance, by the beginning of the war different codes of rugby (league and union) and separate associations governing Australian Rules football served as clear indicators of the effectiveness of the games ethic in crystallizing class distinctions. The Victorian Football Association, the amateur organization, abandoned its competition during the war, as did the organizers of the rugby union competition in Sydney, while the professional Victorian Football League and the Sydney Rugby League competitions continued in the face of mounting hostility from the press and other middle-class spokesmen. In a 1917 edition of the *Bulletin*, one pro-recruitment writer claimed that 'sport and war are rivals, and there is no room for both of them . . . . Every footballer is a possible soldier, so the winter game will have no excuse this year for showing itself in public.'[25]

L.A. Adamson, Headmaster of Wesley College in Melbourne, was a leading figure in support of Australian involvement in defence of the Empire. Cadet training had been a significant part of his system at Wesley, and according to Crawford, he was reputed to have employed 'one of the best military drill instructors in the state'.[26] When the question of enlistment became a reality early in 1914, many of Wesley's former pupils joined up immediately, Adamson celebrating their actions with banquets at the school. His view, expressed on a visit to England in 1912, that sport is 'auxiliary to and in connection with military work', provides a very clear explanation of his role as a leader of the campaign in 1914 to have all sports competitions abandoned for the duration of the war. Adamson 'alleged that any patriotic German in Melbourne would pay to help sustain spectator sport because it so obviously interfered with the recruiting movement', and he banned all Wesley boys from attending professional football matches.[27] Since sport was 'a sound preparation for the battle of life',[28] and since the time had come to put that preparation to the test, there was no point in professional sportsmen continuing to play during the war.[29]

McKernan provides a clear indication of the extent to which the values associated with games playing had been elaborated beyond schooling to become a mark of social distinction more generally. Sport exemplified the values that separated the various strata of the middle classes from those they perceived to be their social and moral inferiors. In times of extreme social stress like war, the disparate class-based values in which the practice of sport was embedded came to the surface. For the middle classes especially, sport exemplified the values that should govern any decent 'civilized' society, and so was ideally suited as an educational medium. But for the working classes, sport was a form of release from social responsibilities and the onerous duties associated with work. McKernan suggests this difference was largely misunderstood by ruling class policy-makers and by many other middle-class Australians, who by 1917 'seemed to believe that a devotion to sport indicated an antipathy or indifference to the real issues of the day'.[30]

At the same time, this attitude 'seems to have baffled the working-class devotees of sport, who took a much more pragmatic approach. Sport was seen more as pleasure and entertainment and in a sense, therefore, not taken as seriously. To suggest that a few hours spent watching a football match induced apathy or indifference to higher struggles or duties seemed silly.'[31] Since the majority of working-class people had never played organized team games in an educational context, these major differences in perspective hardly seem surprising. Until the 1910s, and even then in small numbers, most working-class women would not have played any organized team games at all, and the extent of most men's experience of sport would have been spontaneous *ad hoc* games and spectatorship. When working people did become involved in sport, it was something they played, watched and betted on for fun, not for moral or spiritual upliftment. Following the First World War, this situation began to change as team games increasingly became available to working-class children, their place in schools justified by appeal to reconstructed versions of the games ethic.

Social Distancing and Emulation: Sport and the Games Ethic in Government High Schools

Between 1905 and 1910, the Victorian government established eight state secondary schools, opening the way for the wholesale adoption of the games ethic. According to Bessant, the 'plan was for the child to leave elementary school at the completion of Grade 6 and having passed the qualifying examination (or equivalent), he/she would enter the secondary school'.[32] The Fink Royal Commission which reviewed Victorian government education provision between 1891 and 1901 recommended the appointment of a Director of Education, whose task was to promote schooling for national efficiency. Frank Tate, the first incumbent of this post, believed passionately in this ideal. His ambitious plans included the desire to bring all educational provision under state control and to introduce vocational and technical education for the masses.

While the new high schools intended to offer some courses identical to those available in the private secondary schools, it was assumed by Tate that an industrial course would be most popular among the large numbers of working-class pupils who were expected to take advantage of this opportunity. Very quickly it became clear that this expectation would not be fulfilled. Reacting to pressure from socially ambitious parents for their children's success in public examinations, state high schools soon began to emulate the practices of the elite private schools in every respect. The promotion of sport and the games ethic as its major justification was a prevalent part of this process of social emulation throughout the new high schools.

Far from serving the sons and daughters of the traditional working classes, the schools broadened the opportunities available to the lower ranks of the middle classes to use education as a means of social mobility and exclusiveness. The state high schools charged fees – less than the private institutions but still too high for many working-class parents – a factor that was compounded by the fact that staying on to secondary school meant deferring the possibility of an additional wage in the family. The establishment of government-sponsored secondary schooling in Victoria did little to enhance the class position of more than a handful of working-class individuals, and nothing to dissolve class distinctions. On the contrary, the transplantation of the games ethic to government high schools was consolidated as a strategic practice of social emulation and distancing.

The possibility that the new government high schools might utilize competitive team games to emulate their perceived social superiors was not far-fetched when we consider that these schools were, in several important respects, in competition with some schools in the private system. More surprising, perhaps, is the fact that games playing and the games ethic had already begun to make inroads to the government elementary schools in Victoria and in most other Australian states even before the high schools had been established. Despite the distinctively different cultural orientations of the urban working classes and the middle class and rural groups in Australia indicated by McKernan, the ideals embodied in the public school games ethic can be detected in state elementary schools soon after federation in 1901.

Civilizing Working-Class Bodies:
Team Games in Government Elementary Schools

In Victoria, a State Schools' Amateur Athletics Association (VSSAAA) was formed in June 1904 with 'large numbers of teachers present' in the Melbourne Town Hall.[33] Fifteen teachers, all male, formed the inaugural committee. One daily newspaper, *The Herald*, commented that 'it is a matter for sincere congratulation that the enthusiasm for a representative body of State-school teachers has at last recognised the importance of encouraging the primary schools to compete in interschool matches'.[34] A major motivation behind the establishment of the VSSAAA was the organization of inter-school and inter-state contests in football and cricket for boys. Games were initially strictly extra-curricular, and it was to take almost thirty years before they came to be recognized as an acceptable part of the state primary school curriculum.

There was also some keen nationalist and business motivations behind the establishment of the Association. Reporting on the inaugural meeting of the VSSAAA, *The Herald* commented that an upcoming football match between Victorian and New South Wales schools 'will be of great interest to all connected with football under Australian rules . . . [since] in spite of the strong antagonism of Rugby enthusiasts, there are great possibilities for the Australian game if a proper support is accorded to the State Schools' Amateur Athletic Association'.[35] This role of schools in fostering an Australian version of football was based on the ideal that 'footballers of the future are now at school, and probably the majority of them attend the State schools of Victoria and New South Wales . . . we may rely on these players to continue in the game that they have learned at school, when they become active members of League clubs in either State'. Despite the fact that the VSSAAA was avowedly an organization for amateur sports, representatives of the professional Victorian Football League were in attendance at the inaugural meeting and the VFL gave its 'hearty support' to the enterprise, reflecting their interest in government schools as a recruiting ground for players who might eventually join the senior ranks as professional players.

From the outset, the Victorian government and its Department of Public Instruction provided considerable support to the organization of inter-school and inter-state sport competitions. In October 1904, the *Education Gazette*, an official government publication, reported in some detail the visit to Melbourne of a Petersham State School team, the New South Wales premiership side. The party was greeted amidst considerable pomp and circumstance at Spencer Street Railway Station by Director of Education Frank Tate, whose presence afforded the visit high public prominence. Petersham played the Victorian state school premiership team Albert Park before 20,000 spectators who had come to watch Fitzroy and Carlton contest the VFL Grand Final. While Albert Park lost the match, the *Gazette* reported in a fashion characteristic of accounts of public school matches that the 'lads played splendidly and pluckily, but they were altogether over-matched in size by the Sydney team, who, however, played a manly and a good game'.[36]

A second game against a combined Melbourne state schools team still managed to draw a crowd of 5000 spectators even without the attraction of the senior players. In a deft touch by the VSSAAA, and bearing in mind the amateur status of its youthful players, the proceeds of the second game (about £50) were donated to the Sydney and Melbourne Children's Hospitals. Moreover, the captains of the respective teams, Godbold of Petersham and James of Melbourne, were made life-governors of the hospitals. Revealing their keen interest in the successful establishment of sport in government schools, the VFL president hosted a dinner for both teams, and the guests included delegates from the VFL clubs, Frank Tate, and L.A. Adamson, Headmaster of Wesley College.

While the establishment of extra-curricular sports competitions had the full support and backing of the upper levels of the educational bureaucracies in Victoria and other states, enthusiasm among sections of the teaching profession to assist in the organization of school sport varied from school to school, a matter communicated with some regret by Secretary of the VSSAAA, Mr George Dean. We can see from his report that by 1909, there was also some attention being directed towards the participation of girls.

In some schools, there is an absence of interest in the doings of the boys. Children go to the matches unattended by a teacher and have to coach themselves. In other schools, there are three or four always ready to help the boys. Now that the rounder rules are printed, it is hoped that more women will take an interest in the games. In some schools, women teachers take a keen interest in the game, and at these places the games are always followed by afternoon tea for the players, thus making the games social functions.[37]

Despite this unsurprising mix of responses from teachers and general neglect of girls, there can be little doubt that the provision in government primary and secondary schools of competitive team games from its inception found general support. In practice, however, there were real barriers to participation by anything more than a minority of boys and girls. For instance, the VSSAAA, as we have seen, was primarily concerned with the organization

103

of competitions. There was no provision made for the teaching of games in state elementary schools. Moreover, few teachers would have had the expertise beyond their own experience to teach even the rudiments of the major team games, since none of the teacher training courses of the time recognized games as part of the curriculum.

At least as serious a problem was a lack of facilities and space needed for games, a problem that was shared by the British.[38] Indeed, we are rather forcibly reminded on this point that possession of open spaces for games playing was, as Mangan[39] has noted, a very obvious mark of wealth and privilege, which is one reason why games were so effectively utilized by successive networks of private schools and state high schools as a means of emulation and distancing from institutions higher and lower in the social pecking order. Before the end of the First World War, lack of appropriate facilities for team games in government schools represented a serious barrier to the wider dissemination of the games ethic among the urban working classes, since it was only a minority of pupils who were able to play games.

SCHOOL PLAY-GROUNDS.

TO THE EDITOR OF THE ARGUS.

Sir. – I had occasion to visit the Victoria park State school to-day, and I found there a most incongruous condition of things – a large building in a very small area of ground. The playing space is so small that the boys have no room for free running about, except at peril of injury. Serious accidents through collisions have already happened. Yet, right opposite the school is the spacious area known as the Victoria park recreation ground. This ground is used once or twice a week by a score or two of men playing cricket or football, with the accompanying attendance of spectators. Yet this seldom used reserve may not be used by the scholars opposite, not even by the boys for cricket and football. This seems an anomalous and ridiculous state of affairs. Reserves and recreation grounds are set apart for the good of the community and should be utilised to the greatest possible extent towards that end. Is it not therefore wrong that about 1,000 children should have to play in a small pocket-handkerchief asphalt allotment, surrounded by backyards and sanitary conveniences, while this magnificent ground lies unused week after week? A movement is afoot to open school playgrounds as playing spaces for children of the community. Surely the reserves of the city should be opened up where necessary to the school children in cramped-up schools. – Yours, &c., INTERESTED.[40]

Lack of instruction in games, lack of training and interest among teachers and lack of facilities set limits on the extent to which inter-school sport could progress in Victoria's elementary and high schools. Notwithstanding these limiting factors, the idea that working-class children had a right to play games after the fashion of their socially privileged counterparts had taken firm root in the government education system by the end of the First World War. It was this idea that established the possibility of civilizing working-class children's bodies through schooling.

The Rise of the Games Ethic During the Interwar Years

Following the war, and in a context of deepening economic gloom, increasingly open social conflict and reactionary politics, and profound social pessimism,[41] the arguments most consistently advanced for the expansion of sport in Victorian government schools drew heavily on the games ethic. Mr J.H. Warren, Headmaster of the Horsham High School, who is quoted at the beginning of this chapter, remarked that 'sport has come to stay in the schools'. His comment proved to be prophetic, though his optimism that participation in games would produce the desirable effects he listed was less well founded.

Despite the limitations facing schools,[42] participation rates after the war continued to grow in a widening range of activities, including football, cricket and baseball for boys, and for girls, rounders and women's basketball, and athletics and swimming for both boys and girls.[43] Viewing the elite schools' uses of competitive team games and sport rather uncritically, throughout the 1920s advocates of the amateur ideal consistently argued, in similar fashion to Warren, that children in state schools should have access to the development of the qualities sport purportedly produced in the privileged youth of Australia. This advocacy continued in the face of growing evidence that as sports participation increased, government schools were suffering some of the same excesses of the cult of athleticism as their counterparts in the private system.

Writing in 1925, the Minister of Education in Victoria reported that the VSSAAA was continuing to promote inter-school sports contests with the aim of developing 'a love of sport for its own sake and a subordination of self for the sake of the team'.[44] However, the report acknowledged that it did so in the face of competition having 'a tendency to develop a cult of athleticism'. The lust for victory and the use of sport to legitimate unruly behaviour were becoming increasingly visible in inter-school sport in the government schools. The Minister's report for 1932 suggested that a gap between the amateur ideal and the realities of competitive team sport was not only persisting, but that it was actually widening. The Minister remarked that while representative competition had grown considerably to include more frequent inter-district and inter-state matches in a wider range of games, he felt the need to reiterate the moral and spiritual values of 'wholesome amateur sport' since it was only 'minds filled with the spirit of true play [that] are unsuitable breeding grounds for what is unwholesome'.[45]

These less wholesome aspects of competition were enough to ensure that support for inter-school competition was not unanimous. What had begun as extra-curricular sport was increasingly taking pupils and teachers away from the school during timetabled lessons. In May 1929, and after some years of prevarication, the Victorian Education Department finally issued guidelines advising that pupils' and teachers' involvement in extra-curricular sport at the expense of class work should be minimized. In addition to expressing concern over school time lost to inter-school competition, the Department warned head teachers that pupils should not be permitted to attend sports fixtures unaccompanied. Likewise, some teachers had clearly been using sports fixtures as a means of obtaining illicit time off, with some 'absent during official hours at the recent test match'.[46]

Perhaps it was because of these anomalies between the practice of inter-school sport and the professed values of the games ethic that advocates for games felt the need to make continuing and frequent recourse to the amateur ideal as a justification for games playing in government schools. Within a decade following the end of the First World War, extra-curricular inter-school sport had grown to such prominence in Victoria that the games ethic had begun to exert a powerful influence on conceptions of the nature of physical training offered within the school curriculum. In effect, the games ethic became a large part of the philosophical core of a definition of 'physical education'. As the influence of team games and the ideology in which they were embedded began to be consolidated in government schools, there was a tendency to identify the term 'physical training' as applying narrowly to drilling and exercising, and to refer instead to physical education.

By the end of the 1920s, the Victorian Minister of Education was acknowledging this trend, commenting that physical education 'includes not merely formal physical exercises, but swimming, organized games, rhythmic exercises, folk dancing, practical hygiene, and remedial exercises based on the medical assessment of the needs of each child'.[47] This trend, to acknowledge team games as a legitimate part of the school curriculum and not merely an extra-curricular adjunct, continued. In 1934, the Victorian Education Department formally recognized sport as a legitimate part of the curriculum in its own right, that is, in addition to its incorporation in physical education programmes, and issued advice in its *Course of Study for Schools 1934*, advocating the house system as the best means of stimulating interest in intra-school sport. This system was based on the ideal 'that every child will take part in at least two sports for recreative purposes, and will play in house teams, although he may be unable to qualify for inclusion in the school team'.[48]

Civilized Bodies

While the dominant version of the games ethic in Australia resembled closely the later English version representing 'neo-Spartan virility as exemplified by stoicism, hardiness and endurance',[49] the pressures of the movement towards Australian nationhood and independence between federation in 1901 and the end of the First World War revealed tensions peculiar to Australia's changing place in the British Empire and the world at large. As we have seen in this chapter, there were important contrasts that surfaced during the First World War between middle-class and rural Australian conceptions of competitive teams games, inspired primarily by the games ethic, and the professionalism and pragmatism of the urban working-class view of competitive sport. Each group's approach to sport reflected contrasting world views.

In this context, justifications for competitive sport in government schools between federation and the end of the Second World War that drew heavily on sentiments constituting the games ethic may have been of questionable relevance to working-class children. There were a number of interests at work in promoting these justifications, and a range of possible explanations for the consolidation of a version of the games ethic in schools for the working classes. Professional sports organizations, such as the Victorian Football League, considered government schools to be an important recruiting ground for their sports. Socially aspiring groups within the government system, such as the clientele of the high schools, used games as a means of social emulation and distancing. In addition to this use of games as a symbol of social elitism, it might be argued that there was a motive on the part of ruling groups to use games as civilizing devices, as a means of producing civilized bodies among the working classes of Australia. This goal began to emerge as a reality as a reconstructed version of the games ethic could reach all children through mass schooling and the new physical education, a matter we turn to in the next chapter.

When the federal government withdrew support for the Department of Defence's involvement in the organization of school physical training in 1929, the state governments were initially thrown into confusion. However, the end of the military's involvement presented an opportunity for new developments that the emerging civilian physical education profession in Australia grasped enthusiastically. As we will see in the next chapter, the growing prominence of competitive team games in government schools, facilitated by a National Fitness Act of 1941 that firmly established mass physical recreation as the dominant discourse in physical culture, had a profound influence in defining a new form of physical education that seemed to promise the schooling of liberated bodies.

Notes and References

1 Mr J.H. Warren, Headmaster of the Horsham High School, in Victorian Education Department *Education Gazette and Teachers' Aid*, August 1919, p. 128.
2 See Hargreaves, J.A. (1985) 'Playing Like Gentlemen While Behaving Like Ladies': Contradictory Features of the Formative Years of Women's Sport *The British Journal of Sport History*, **2**, pp. 40–52; and Young, L. (1984) Feminism and the physical: sex education, physical education and dress reform in Victoria, 1880–1930. Unpublished MA Thesis, Monash University.
3 Mangan, J.A. (1986) *The Games Ethic and Imperialism: Aspects of the Diffusion of an Ideal* Harmondsworth: Viking, p. 18.
4 Mangan, *The Games Ethic*, pp. 142–65.
5 Mangan, J.A. (1983) Grammar schools and the games ethic in Victorian and Edwardian eras *Albion*, **15**, p. 330; see Kirk, D. (1992) *Defining Physical Education: The Social Construction of a School Subject in Postwar Britain* London: Falmer for an account of the reconstruction of the games ethic for use in British government secondary schools after the Second World War.
6 The term 'middle classes' is used here in preference to bourgeoisie to denote the contrasting constitutions of the social groups in Britain who used the elite schools as a means of social demarcation, and the groups in Australia who used the public and grammar schools for similar purposes. It should be noted, nevertheless, that the various strata of the Australian middle classes are linked through their use of education as a key strategy of social aspiration, and that these schools and this varied class grouping supplied a disproportionately larger number of religious, social, political, economic and miltary leaders than the working classes. See Connell, R. and Irving, T. (1982) 'Yes, Virginia, there is a ruling class', in Mayer, H. and Nelson, H. (eds) *Australian Politics: A Fifth Reader* Melbourne: Longman Cheshire.
7 Sherington, G. (1983) Athleticism in the Antipodes: the AAGPS of New South Wales *History of Education Review*, **12**, pp. 16–28.
8 Sherington, Athleticism in the Antipodes, p. 21.
9 *Argus*, 27 January 1934.
10 Crawford, R. (1986) Athleticism, gentlemen and Empire in Australian public schools: L.A. Adamson and Wesley College, Melbourne, in *Sport & Colonialism in 19th Century Australasia* Adelaide: ASSH, pp. 42–64.
11 Bean, C.E.W. (1950) *Here, My Son: An Account of the Independent and Other Corporate Boys' Schools of Australia* Sydney: Angus and Robertson, p. 168.
12 See Mangan, Grammar schools and the games ethic. We should note, along with Bean, one important difference between the Australian adoption of games to fulfil this purpose, and practice in the English setting. The formation of associations to organize sport in Australian elite schools contrasted with the English practice of school matches being arranged between individual schools. Australian school

sports associations also established premiership competitions, which were studiously avoided by their English counterparts, see Bean *Here, My Son*, p. 169.

13 See the *Argus*, 27 January 1934.

14 Dening, G. (1978) *Xavier – A Centenary Portrait* Kew, Vic.: Old Xaverians' Association, p. 178.

15 Cf. Smith, W.D. (1974) *Stretching Their Bodies: The History of Physical Education* London: David & Charles, pp. 54–8.

16 Crawford, R. (1984) Sport for young ladies: The Victorian independent schools 1875-1925 *Sporting Traditions: The Journal of the Australian Society for Sports History*, **1**, pp. 61–82.

17 Bessant, R. (1984) The influence of the 'Public Schools' on the early high schools of Victoria *History of Education Review*, **13**, pp. 45–57.

18 School poem from the Tintern School, Melbourne *c.* 1920, in Gardiner, L. (1977) *Tintern School and Anglican Girls' Education 1877–1977* Melbourne: Wilkie, p. 77.

19 Gardiner, *Tintern School*, p. 26.

20 Wright, J. (1996) Mapping the discourses in physical education *Journal of Curriculum Studies*, **28** (3), pp. 331–51.

21 In *The Brook*, the Tintern School magazine, August 1918, quoted by Gardiner, *Tintern School*, p. 79.

22 While it can be argued with some confidence that the values associated with the games ethic had wide currency by the beginning of the twentieth century, there were nevertheless vocal opponents of the excesses of games playing and the use of the values associated with games as a means of legitimating or enobling what were, at times, clearly questionable activities. For a useful qualification of this point, see Brown, D.W. (1988) Criticisms against the value-claim for sport and physical ideal in late nineteenth-century Australia *Sporting Traditions: The Journal of the Australian Society for Sports History*, **4**, pp. 150–61.

23 McKernan, M. (1979) Sport, war and society: Australia 1914–18, in Cashman, R. and McKernan, M. (eds) *Sport in History* St. Lucia: University of Queensland Press, pp. 1–20.

24 McKernan, Sport, war and society, p. 1.

25 McKernan, Sport, war and society, p. 10.

26 Crawford, Athleticism, gentleman and empire, p. 56.

27 McKernan, Sport, war and society, p. 5.

28 Bessant, The influence of the 'Public Schools', p. 53.

29 McKernan suggests that 'as the opinion makers in Australia began to arrogate patriotism exclusively to the bosom of their own class to deny that the Australian worker was instinctively patriotic, they looked with disfavour on his recreations, implying that while such recreations might be innocent amongst a class that recognized its higher duty, they were definitely dangerous among people blinded to that duty', in McKernan, Sport, war and society, p. 11.

30 McKernan, Sport, war and society, p. 17.

31 McKernan, Sport, war and society, p. 18.

32 Bessant, The influence of the 'Public Schools', p. 50.

33 Victorian Education Department *Education Gazette and Teachers' Aid*, July 1904.

34 *The Herald*, 29 June 1904.

35 *The Herald*, 29 June 1904.

36 Victorian Education Department *Education Gazette and Teachers' Aid*, October 1904.
37 Minister of Public Instruction (1909) *Education Report for the Year 1908–9* Melbourne: Government Printer, p. 70.
38 Cf. Smith, *Stretching Their Bodies*; and Kirk, *Defining Physical Education*.
39 Mangan, Grammar schools and the games ethic.
40 *Argus*, 15 May 1913, p. 15.
41 Cf. Macintyre, S. (1986) *The Oxford History of Australia (Volume 4): The Succeeding Age, 1901–1942* Melbourne: Oxford University Press.
42 Older inner-city schools continued to suffer from lack of space in which to play games well into the 1920s and beyond; see, for example, a report in the *Argus*, 1 August 1929, p. 15.
43 Regular, typically positive and optimistic, reports of the progress being made in the provision of games in government schools appear in the Victorian Parliamentary Papers, Reports of the Minister of Public Instruction, through the period from 1920 to 1935.
44 Minister of Public Instruction (1925) *Education Report for the Year 1924–25* Melbourne: Government Printer, p. 7.
45 Minister of Public Instruction (1932) *Education Report for the Year 1931–2* Melbourne: Government Printer, p. 50.
46 Victorian Education Department *Education Gazette and Teachers' Aid*, May 1929.
47 Minister of Public Instruction (1929) *Education Report for the Year 1928–9* Melbourne: Government Printer, p. 8.
48 Victorian Education Department *Education Gazette and Teachers' Aid*, November 1933, p. 498.
49 Crawford, R. (1981) A history of physical education in Victoria and New South Wales 1872–1939: with particular reference to English precedent. Unpublished PhD Thesis, La Trobe University.

6

Liberating Bodies: National Fitness and the New Physical Education

Formal exercises are artificial, unrelated to life situations, and generally lacking in interest; they also completely ignore the very important influence that the emotions exert on the physical well-being of the individual. Enjoyment and enthusiasm are necessary if the exercise is to have a stimulating and beneficial effect. We therefore insist that every child has the right to play, and that this right must be restored to all children who have lost it.[1]

It is clear that governments cannot make individuals healthy and cannot – at least under existing conditions – compel the community to make itself physically fit . . . . It is therefore for the government to take advantage of the spirit which is manifesting itself on a universal scale and provide facilities for greatly extended activities.[2]

The shift in public discourse that provided Dr Kelly and Senator Foll with the language and the rationale for making these statements had its source both in new and influential thinking about education promoted by advocates for child-centred methods, and in the national fitness movement that championed the cause of healthy physical recreation for the masses. In these statements we can detect something of the nature of this emerging shift in thinking about the body as a site of social regulation. In contrast to the 'heavy, ponderous and meticulous' exercise of power evident in drilling and medical inspection, Kelly and Foll seem to be using a language describing 'a looser form of power' over the body. Individuals cannot be compelled to become physically fit, the desire to do so can only be encouraged through the provision of the facilities and opportunities for mass recreation. Part of this process of encouragement is to see physical exercise as enjoyable, and where children's natural enthusiasm to be physically active has been suppressed, this enthusiasm must be restored as a right.

The shift away from coersive forms of drilling and meticulous medical examination to more liberal practices centred on schooling bodies was, as we saw in the previous chapter, signalled by the growing influence of competitive team games in government schools. Indeed, as we will see later in this chapter in an elaboration of Dr Kelly's 1946 statement, there was a willingness to equate 'play', as a 'natural impulse' of childhood, with playing competitive team games, to an extent that a reader might have been led to the view that it was playing team games that was somehow 'natural' and a right of all children. In the campaign for national fitness that had its outcome in the 1941 National Fitness Act, fitness for defence was consciously downplayed by federal politicians while strenuous efforts were made to link national fitness to health and general well-being.

While there is in these emerging discourses some clear emancipatory intent to liberate bodies from earlier, relatively more coersive and oppressive regimes of practice, we should not lose sight of the regulative imperatives that remained within the institutions of schooling, defence and public health. Schools continued to face many of the same challenges as their nineteenth-century predecessors, chief among them the need for the dual attributes of compliance and productivity from pupils. And as we will see, some of the advocates for a national fitness campaign in Australia were motivated less by the desire to liberate bodies as by enduring concerns over the deterioration of the race and the fitness of the nation for defence. Overseas developments in the area of mass physical recreation, particularly the influence of Germany's use of physical activities in its youth movement and the effects of these developments on Britain, were important points of reference for Australian citizens and politicians. Within this context of international developments, this chapter documents the shifts in public discourse towards a looser form of power to liberate bodies, through the national fitness campaign of the 1930s, and through some of the consequences of this campaign for mass physical culture and for sport-centred school physical education during and after the war.

The National Fitness Campaign

The campaign that led to the 1941 National Fitness Act had begun in the mid-1930s and had many contributors.[3] We noted in Chapter 4 that the federal government had suspended indefinitely the compulsory military training scheme in 1929, and with it junior cadet training and the Department of Defence's support for physical training in schools. The states were left with the task of filling the gap this withdrawal of support had left. The problem lay not so much in a lack of commitment to organized physical activity in schools, which as we saw in Chapters 2 and 5 seemed to enjoy widespread support, but in the question of funding.

The funding of school physical training had always been a bone of contention between the federal government and the states, and their relative contribution to funding was again to feature large in the campaign for national fitness. This issue was first among others in delaying the federal government's response to the mounting pressure from a variety of lobby groups for action on national fitness. A cartoon in the Melbourne *Age*, published during Health Week in August 1938, portrays in an inset a variety of these organizations as athletes keenly waiting, on 31 May 1938, at the starting line for the signal from the starter, the federal government. In the main part of the cartoon, the athletes are (some three months later) in various conditions of weariness and frustration as the starter, now cobweb festooned, remains in the same position, poised to fire the pistol.[4] The states, for their part, seemed always reluctant to fund any service that might be funded from elsewhere, while jealously guarding their control over such constitutional responsibilities as education.[5]

An important early contribution to the push for a national fitness campaign was initiated in 1935, when the National Council of Women in Victoria and the Australian Council for Educational Research sponsored a survey of physical education provision in Victoria.[6] One of their aims was to discover whether it might be possible to establish training courses for specialist teachers of physical education. Colonel Alan Ramsay, Master of Method in Education at the University of Melbourne and Meg Johnson, diplomate of Bedford College and the physical education teacher at the Emily McPherson College in Melbourne, were appointed to conduct the survey. In the foreword to the Ramsay and Johnson report, G.S. Browne, Professor of Education at Melbourne University, noted that Germany and Italy had 'laid great emphasis on physical education, but have given it a strong militaristic bias', while Britain had just announced the inauguration of a mass physical recreation scheme 'with the direct aim of improving the health and physique of her people'. This survey was intended to contribute to the initiation of a similar scheme in Australia, by mapping the provision of school physical education in Victoria.

Ramsay and Johnson discovered that the larger private schools for girls employed full-time specialist teachers of physical education, who offered instruction in games and gymnastics, while the schools for boys tended to rely on extra-curricular participation in competitive team games as the main form of physical activity. The situation in the government elementary and secondary schools was patchy, with sport organized by volunteers as an extra-curricular activity and instruction in swimming and physical exercise depending on the expertise and enthusiasm of the class teachers, since the two organizers in physical education and one in swimming were stretched to the limit following the final withdrawal of the Defence Department staff in 1931.

On the basis of their review, published late in 1935, Ramsay and Johnson strongly supported the establishment of a specialist training course for teachers of physical education based at the University of Melbourne, a recommendation that the University acted on promptly, due largely to the efforts of Professor Browne. Ironically, it was only possible to establish this course because of one German Jew's persecution and the benevolence of the Carnegie Corporation. The Carnegie Corporation were in 1936 attempting to find employment for Germans exiled by Hitler's regime. Following considerable negotiation, Dr Fritz Duras, a medical practitioner and sport scientist who had been dismissed in 1934 from his post at the University of Frieberg due to his Jewish ancestry, was appointed Director of the new course in physical education, his salary to be paid for two years by the Corporation. The course began initially as a one-year certificate programme, but it was so popular with students that midway through 1937 Duras successfully negotiated with the University Council for a further year of study towards a diploma. Around ten full-time students enrolled in the course in 1937, along with a further twenty or so practising teachers who enrolled part-time.[7]

The subject matter of this first-ever course in physical education to be offered by an Australian university was aimed squarely at teaching and reflected a profoundly European influence. In the content of the course, we can see evidence of the shift in practices, away from regimentation to a more liberal regime, though the knowledge base considered appropriate to teaching physical education was predominately scientific and involved a mix of academic study and practical physical experience. Duras taught the anatomical and physiological bases of human movement, students studied physics and chemistry with Alan Ramsay, the author of the 1935 report, while his co-author, Meg Johnson, and a host of other part-time staff or staff from other departments of the University offered instruction in body mechanics, gymnastics, principles and methods of physical education, games, fencing, athletics and dancing. The notion that schooling bodies should also be fun was reflected in the addition of activities such as camping, trail-riding, skiing and youth hostelling.[8] Nowhere was there mention of marching, squad drill or rifle shooting.

There was support for university-trained physical education teachers from a variety of sources,[9] and a recognition by some that Australia had lagged behind the rest of the international community in this field. In Britain, privately run colleges for training women gymnasts had been in existence since the 1890s. While some, such as Dunfermline College in Scotland, did accept men, the numbers of trained male teachers were small compared with women. Specialist colleges for men opened in Glasgow, Leeds and

114

Loughborough in the early to mid-1930s, though men were to remain in the minority of trained physical educators until the 1960s, their small numbers offset only by the high attrition of women from the workforce.[10]

While Australia may have lagged well behind Britain in the training of women, though not so much in the training of men, none of the single-sex specialist colleges in Britain at this time offered students the experience of a university education, and in this Australia was ahead of Britain and closer to the American model, where physical education had been well established in universities. Indeed, it was to the American experience the historian C.E.W. Bean was alluding when he wrote to Dr Cumpston, Commonwealth Director-General of Health in June 1937 that 'we here in Sydney have been trying for years to get the training of sports masters and mistresses and those in charge of the physical training of youth put on a higher basis than that of the old physical drill instructor. For years some of us have contended that this profession is worthy of a university training and if Froebel's great principle of education through play was to be put into practice it required a fine type of brain and culture as well as mere physical skill and development.'[11] Following the precedent set by the University of Melbourne, Bean's views and those of other advocates, including Professor Browne,[12] had a clear outcome in the National Fitness Act through the provision of federal government funds to establish courses in physical education at each of the other Australian universities.

The pressure on the federal government to act on the question of national fitness increased during 1938 as growing tension in Europe suggested that war could be imminent. Questions had been raised in federal Parliament as early as December 1936 concerning the possibility of establishing a scheme that would improve the level of national fitness.[13] In 1937, Billy Hughes, architect of the Immigration Restriction Act of 1902, former Prime Minister and now federal Minister for Health, told Parliament that the nation faced a crisis: 'We, the descendants of one of the most vigorous, active and adventurous races, lead sedentary lives, take little corrective exercise and live on devitalized food.'[14] Hughes set aside funds for health research to be administered by a newly created National Health and Medical Research Council (NH&MRC). The first grants to the NH&MRC were approved late in 1937 and in 1938 the NH&MRC endorsed a series of resolutions concerning national fitness. It noted the increasing complexity of the international situation, the worrying implications of a declining birth rate, particularly in the cities, and 'lower standards of personal and national efficiency than were consistent with self respect. The foremost medical body in the country had declared that Australia was trying to maintain its place in a competitive world with a jaded, maladapted and inefficient population.'[15]

For at least two years before the federal government formally instituted a national fitness campaign through the offices of the NH&MRC, there were a large number of organizations actively pursuing national fitness goals. The New South Wales government was involved early in these developments and had formed a Physical Education Advisory Committee in 1937.[16] In Victoria, the *Age* newspaper was vocal in promoting the need for a national fitness campaign and went as far as proposing how the campaign might work. In its issue of 16 May 1938, the *Age* reported that the Prime Minister, Mr Lyons, had 'expressed his belief in the wisdom of such a campaign'.[17] The newspaper claimed there was widespread interest in its scheme, suggesting that 'the readiness and enthusiasm with which public individuals and institutions are looking forward to a practical lead from the government are reminiscent of the unanimity that characterised the British scheme'. The *Age*'s view was that 'with physical fitness now generally recognised as a matter of national duty as well as one of individual right, a nation wide scheme must develop from national government encouragement and assistance'. The plan was for 'a Federal Council for allocating grants and directing policy with local committees controlling the sports centres in cities and towns and making sound use of subsidies that would be available for the provision of necessary facilities'.

A number of other individuals and organizations expressed their views on the topic of national fitness. Echoing eugenicists' arguments, the Australian Natives Association deplored the lack of organized effort 'to raise the physical fitness of the Australian race'.[18] The Baptist Union of Tasmania urged that greater attention must be paid to physical education in schools, while the Council of Churches in Victoria commended the *Age* on its support for a national fitness campaign.[19] C.E.W. Bean offered advice on overseas models for an Australian campaign,[20] while the Australian Youth Council urged that any proposed national fitness scheme should operate through existing youth organizations.[21] In July 1938, physical culturist Mr T.A. Langridge advanced to the government a five-year plan for national fitness,[22] the Recreation and Leadership Movement organized a conference in August that proposed national fitness to be a key requirement of Education and Good Citizenship,[23] and later that month the Australian Teachers' Federation passed unanimously a resolution to promote physical culture throughout Australia.[24] The Health Association of Australasia had also prepared a plan for a national fitness campaign that it submitted to the federal government in late October.[25]

Despite this advice and encouragement from the public, the federal government's own ideas on the desirability and nature of a national fitness campaign seemed to be slow in forming. In response to questions raised in Parliament in May 1938, the Prime Minister confirmed his support for a national fitness campaign reported in the *Age* three days previously.[26] The

NH&MRC had been given responsibility by the Lyons government for formulating a plan for national fitness, but during a debate in the House of Representatives in June the issue seemed to centre around diet rather than physical activity. In a policy speech to the House, the Prime Minister claimed that 'Australia needs not only a numerous but a virile population and virility is very largely a matter of proper feeding . . . . The government last year appointed a Nutrition Committee to inquire into and report upon the food of our people in relation to health and throughout this year has conducted a massive campaign for the purpose of educating the community on questions relating to diet. We will follow up any recommendations made by the Advisory Council on Nutrition and the National Health and Medical Research Council.'[27]

Contrasting with these views, in October the Melbourne *Argus* reported that details of a national fitness campaign were being prepared by the department of the Director-General of Public Health in NSW, Dr E. Sydney Morris, and these plans were expected to be endorsed by the National Health and Medical Research Council at their conference in November.[28] When the Prime Minister received the NH&MRC's report embracing Morris's plan, he was reported by the *Argus* to have said that the federal government was taking the proposals 'very seriously' and that the preparation of plans to improve national fitness would be discussed at the Conference of State Premiers. Significantly this conference was being held to hear a review of the government's defence strategies in which national fitness was to play a key role.[29]

The *Argus*'s rival newspaper in Melbourne, the *Age*, had no doubt that the plans would be endorsed by the State Premiers and had reported triumphantly a day earlier on 17 November that its plan for national fitness had been adopted.

Unqualified endorsement of the plan to commence a national fitness campaign in Australia has been given by the NH&MRC which concluded its meeting at Canberra today. The scheme's proposal follows the lines suggested by the *Age*. The Federal government has been recommended to form immediately a National Council of Physical Fitness to invite the cooperation of the State governments in forming Councils and to urge local governing bodies to make available playgrounds, sports fields, swimming pools and other tangible equipment and facilities. The Minister for Health Senator Foll announced subsequently that he would consider the report and make recommendations to Cabinet. The Council which consists of the Chiefs of the Health Departments of the Commonwealth and States and representative laymen expressed itself as being 'convinced of the urgency and importance of establishing a national organisation which shall have as its main objective a standard of physical fitness such as this country with its racial heritages, natural environment and economic opportunities should show'.[30]

The Council's strong words on the state of the Australian population hinted at a re-emergence of the perennial eugenic concern of racial deterioration. Under a headline of 'True National Fitness', the editorial in the 3 December issue of the *Argus* newspaper reverted to the familiar argument that the unfit and mentally defective were out-breeding the 'clean limbed people with sound minds in sound bodies' and quoted with approval comments to this effect by a visiting English physician, Sir Bruce Bruce-Porter, who gloomily predicted that 'if these tendencies persist it is inevitable that civilisation has in it the principle of decay and that the human race is heading for the slope'. At the same time the editorial hearkened back to the same anxiety that had possessed people after the publication of Coghlan's report of declining birth rates in Australia in 1903. The editor argued that 'national fitness is something more than the physical fitness of individuals. There can be none in a country where there is a failure to retain its population and even to increase the number of its people.'[31] By 1938 the high levels of physical efficiency obtained by totalitarian states such as Germany were widely known, discussed and often openly admired and this created a new edge to calls for a national fitness campaign. Here was a tangible example of what could be achieved. The *Argus* editorial verged dangerously close to endorsing this approach in posing the question 'is individual freedom – or the greatest measure of it – consistent with national fitness?' The editor's answer was that 'supremacy is being asserted if not actually attained in Europe by those nations that demand of individuals complete service in the cause of national fitness. Government is in this conception an instrument to promote the welfare of the people so that the people may contribute to the strength of government. Apparently that appeal – or that command – has an efficacy that has not been so far apparent in those countries where freedom includes the right to discipline oneself as distinct from the duty to be disciplined by the state.'

Cabinet took less than three weeks to agree to the proposals for a national fitness campaign, the 'unusual rapidity' of decision making due, according to the *Sydney Sun*, to 'the energy with which the Minister for Health, Senator Foll, has tackled a problem which he regards as one calling for an urgent solution'.[32] But just what it was, precisely, Cabinet had agreed to in the name of national fitness had yet to be clearly defined. There existed a range of interpretations. Many seemed concerned that a national fitness campaign was intended to increase physical fitness at the expense of 'the higher human attributes'.[33] A correspondent to the *Argus* accused the National Fitness Council of adopting a 'purely veterinary attitude to health and fitness' and said she had gained the impression that the 'objective of the campaign is to promote the development of the Australian people as healthy livestock'. She alleged the campaign had ignored the fact that many physically healthy people suffered from disabling mental and emotional disorders.[34] The re-emergence of a eugenicist agenda added a particular twist to the fact that the campaign was to operate under the direction of the Minister for Health and that the primary outcome of the campaign was to be an improvement of the health of Australians in which work on the body was to feature large. Australia's recent experience of militarized physical training and the increasing prospect of war in Europe gave hope to advocates of another, not entirely unrelated, agenda, which was to use physical training as a key means of preparing a defence force.

In November 1938, the Returned Services League argued strongly for compulsory military training in schools, closely followed in January 1939 by the Australian Natives Association who demanded that the government reintroduce the Junior Cadet Training Scheme.[35] Adding to the voices of these two highly influential pressure groups were private citizens like Mr J.J. Stanley, whose letter to the *Argus* in March 1939 urged the government to 'have the courage to adopt compulsory physical training which should be continued and combined with military training for defence purposes after leaving school'.[36] Wary of prompting accusations of militarism or to be too closely associated with the national fitness schemes of the Fascist governments of Germany and Italy, none of the members of the new National Fitness Council specifically linked the national fitness campaign with a defence campaign. Yet to many people the connection was obvious. Addressing the Federation of Mothers' Clubs Conference, President Mrs McNaughton supported the launching of a national fitness campaign in conjunction with a defence campaign and commented that 'the greatest crime against our children would be to be unprepared in a time of war'.[37]

Support for linking the national fitness campaign to compulsory military training also came from the Empire Youth Movement of Australia who claimed in a letter from the organization's secretary to Senator Foll 'to have done more to have brought about the feeling present in the minds of the public today as to the necessity for national fitness than any other individual body'. The purpose of the letter was to request a share of the funds from the proposed federal grant. The secretary identified himself as 'a serving officer of the Defence forces' and claimed to have been in touch with the National Fitness Council in England and to be in possession of their plan 'which we have modified to suit Australian conditions'. The Empire Youth Movement were fully aware of 'the very close connection between national fitness and defence while certain other interests which are striving to control the national fitness campaign are definitely opposed to defence in all its forms'. Senator Foll was also informed of the organization's fundamental beliefs, one of which was 'that all forms of dictatorship are abhorrent to Australian ideals and sentiment and that British democracy is the only form of government that allows us individual liberty and expression'.[38] The Empire Youth Movement's secretary evidently failed to notice the striking similarity between his support for linking national fitness and military training and the uses to which mass physical training were being put by Hitler and Mussolini.

The very delicate issues involved in proposing a national fitness campaign in this context can be seen in the care and diplomacy employed by the federal government in its correspondence with the public. The Western Australia Agent-General in London, drawing on the British experience of promoting national fitness, sent strong advice to Senator Foll not to mention defence in promoting national fitness, and to emphasize instead the well-being of children.[39] Even though the campaign was to be administered by the Commonwealth Department of Health, the tensions between militarism and health as outcomes of a national fitness campaign seemed to be keenly felt by the medical profession itself. The example of what totalitarian states could apparently achieve in schooling the bodies of their young people held an uneasy attraction for those who took a predominantly eugenic approach to the question of national fitness.

Eugenicist and former school medical inspector Harvey Sutton, in an address to a conference of Rhodes Scholars in 1939, commented on 'the progress made on the side of physical education in the totalitarian States', and while 'people of democratic leanings may disapprove of the objects for which the youth of Germany and Italy are being physically trained ... they are forced to recognise that the Fascists have achieved greater national fitness and, as a direct result, greater national effectiveness'.[40] The *Medical Journal of Australia* also felt obliged to speak out on this issue, commenting in August 1938 that the *Age* newspaper article had avoided mentioning the military aspects of physical training, 'but if youth has hope and a stake in the country it should surely be a matter of honour that he make himself physically fit to take his place with older men in the defence of his country'. The editor noted that the 'improvement in the physical fitness of young Germany has made a deep impression on other nations', including Britain. While the *MJA* felt that the notion of breeding a pure Aryan race was 'scientifically unsound', at least it 'had the effect of creating a national pride'.[41]

The Commonwealth Council for National Fitness

The Commonwealth Council for National Fitness began its work in January 1939 within the following context: the renewed interest in eugenics, tension between definitions of national fitness for health or for war, more than a little public sympathy with the effectiveness of German and Italian initiatives in this field, and a reasonable level of public interest in a national fitness campaign. In this complex environment, made more complex by a divided federal coalition government, the death of the Prime Minister in office between its first and second meetings, and an eventual change of government in October 1941,[42] the naming of the Council and its remit were in themselves highly controversial issues. A name change from the Commonwealth or National Coordinating Council for Physical Fitness to the Commonwealth Council for National Fitness mooted at the second meeting may have served two functions. The first was to downplay any militarist agenda for the work of the Council, and the second to force the Council to take a broader view of its role, encompassing not only physical activity, but also the changing health needs of individuals across the life span, the importance of good nutrition, and reflecting concerns over the falling birth rate, 'the adequate care and feeding of the expectant and nursing mother'.[43]

The minutes of the inaugural meeting had included an attachment from the Conference of the New South Wales Public Schools Teachers' Federation consisting of recommendations for the provision of school physical education, sport and swimming that were to be passed on to State Councils once they had been formed, and a summary of recommendations of a Committee on Scottish Health Services that dealt with matters of medical inspection and health education. In this information and in the objectives this first meeting of the Council set for themselves, it is clear that they considered schools to be a primary site of intervention on behalf of national fitness and work on the bodies of children to be the central focus of these interventions. Reporting to Cabinet on the outcomes of this first meeting of the Council, Foll highlighted two issues for immediate action. The first was that state governments should be invited to form State Councils. The second was that lectureships in physical education should be established in each of the six state universities. Foll commented that establishment of training courses and a steady supply of trained teachers was considered essential to the success of the national fitness campaign.[44]

In opening the inaugural meeting Senator Foll was reported by the *Argus* to have remarked that Australia's movement toward a national fitness campaign was in accord with similar movements overseas that promoted a philosophy of wide participation. Throughout the world, he said, there had been 'concerted action to encourage people to play games rather than to look on while someone else played them. Hardly a government was not putting national fitness to the forefront of its policy.' However, in marked contrast to earlier official speeches, when a conspicuous silence was maintained on the connection between national fitness and defence, Senator Foll also stated that national fitness was inseparably bound up with defence.[45] For the first time, the use of the national fitness campaign for military purposes had appeared on the official government agenda.

References to a military agenda did not disappear under the chairmanship of the new Minister for Health Sir Frederick Stewart, although any possibility that this agenda might dominate the Council's work was dispelled by the decision to change the name of the Council and by the resolutions of the second meeting in May 1939, which were much more broad ranging than those of the first. To those first set of resolutions, the Council added the issues of workplace health and safety, medical, dental and nursing services to school children, and re-emphasized the importance of nutritional education and the care of mothers, suggesting in this latter case that 'means should be found to give women for a fortnight in each year change and rest from family and household cares'.[46]

By the third meeting of the Council on 27 July in Melbourne, the deliberations had shifted away from the question of the proper substantive concerns of the Council to the question of funding, and in these deliberations Sir Frederick Stewart played a leading role. Some months earlier, the Prime Minister Mr Lyons had expressed some concerns about the federal government's financial commitment to the campaign to his Minister for Health, Senator Foll, following the dispatch in early January of letters of invitation to the state governments to form State Councils. Later that month, Foll wrote to reassure the Prime Minister that there was considerable support from the states and that apart from the grants to the universities to establish lectureships, and 'from the small cost of fares and out of pocket expenses for which funds have already been provided there should be little expense incurred'.[47] However, some of the states did not necessarily concur with Foll's view, with the Premier of South Australia writing to inform the Prime Minister that his government would be pleased to cooperate with the scheme, but that 'some expense will be involved in regard to the organisation and as such fitness of the citizens of the Commonwealth appears to be definitely a function of your government'.[48]

When the Prime Minister Joseph Lyons died in office in April, Robert Menzies won the contest to be the new Prime Minister and leader of the federal Coalition government.[49] When the government settled back to work in May, it appeared that they intended to persevere with the plan to provide only the grants to the universities.[50] Concerns were expressed by the Victorian Council for Physical Fitness in June that the campaign would come to nothing unless the federal government provided funds.[51] However, the State Council in Victoria had managed to upset members of the state government by requesting funding for services that several Victorian government departments already provided. The *Age* reported that 'most state ministers are not, in fact, sympathetic to the campaign' suggesting that 'it is starting at the wrong end' and any Federal funding would be better spent on educating mothers on the nutritional needs of their children.

In the face of this less than welcoming response from some sections of state governments, the federal government were understandably cautious about their financial commitment to the campaign. However, on the advice of Stewart, who drew heavily on the NH&MRC's endorsement of the Council's recommendations for funding, the government finally made a commitment before the third meeting of the Council of £100,000 over a five-year period, with £20,000 to be spent each year. Stewart's suggestions to the third meeting of the Council regarding the allocation of this money centred on the funding of lectureships or scholarships in each of the universities, the establishment of an organizer of national fitness in each state, and the balance to be spent at his discretion, were accepted unanimously after some discussion by members of the Council. In his comments introducing this proposal, he made clear that the federal government had a delimited role in promoting the national fitness campaign, and that there was an expectation that state and local governments would make a contribution in kind to the work of the State Councils.[52] Commenting on these recommendations in a minute to Cabinet, Stewart suggested that Australian funding was small indeed when compared to that of other countries. He noted that:

> As sponsors we must be prepared to assume an appropriate measure of financial responsibility. We can hardly claim that an aggregate of £18,000 spread over three years and distributed between six states fulfils that obligation in this respect. I recommend therefore that the Coordinating Council's recommendations be approved . . . . In the United Kingdom the government has made provision for a scheme of physical training and recreation involving an expenditure of two million pounds spread over a period of three years and in addition a continued annual charge of £150,000 . . . the government of South Africa has approved an allocation of £50,000 toward a nationalist scheme of PE. In New Zealand, under the New Zealand Physical Welfare and Recreation Act, 1937 the Minister for Internal Affairs authorised from time to time, to make grants to local authorities and voluntary organisations towards the expenses incurred in PT and Recreation.[53]

By the time war was declared in September 1939, State Councils for National Fitness had been established in New South Wales, Victoria, Queensland, Western Australia and Tasmania, with South Australia following suit one month later. Funds had been expended to appoint national and state Organizers of National Fitness. Grants to establish lectureships in physical education were readily accepted by the University of Melbourne, which no longer needed to rely on the benevolence of the Carnegie Corporation to maintain Fritz Duras, and the Universities of Queensland, Adelaide and Sydney, while Tasmania and Western Australia accepted the grants as scholarships to send local students to courses in the other universities. The State Councils were very quickly busy reviewing existing facilities and services, organizing camps, volunteer training courses and flying squads of teachers to tour schools and offer instruction in physical education and sport.[54]

The National Fitness Act passed by federal Parliament in 1941 merely confirmed developments in mass physical recreation that were by then well under way. At the second reading of the Bill in June of that year, Sir Frederick Stewart noted that while in wartime fitness for survival was a prominent concern, he acknowledged the pre-war origins of the Act in his comment that 'we must not forget the ultimate goal of fitness is in order to enjoy life'.[55] Since the Act consolidated work that was being carried out by a range of organizations, the national and state Organizers of National Fitness were quickly into their stride and by the mid-1940s were meeting regularly for the purposes of refining policies and developing strategies.[56]

As we have seen, there was an attempt at the second meeting of the Commonwealth Council for National Fitness to establish a broad agenda for the Council's work that went beyond physical activity. However, it became increasingly clear as the State Councils got under way that the majority of the work associated with national fitness was being done through physical activity programmes in schools and other organizations concerned with children and youth. At the eighth session of the National Council held in Melbourne in October 1945, there was serious and lengthy discussion of proposals from the state representatives to relocate the work of the National Fitness Organizers from departments of health to departments of education.[57] The state representatives noted the recent British decision to shift responsibility for school physical training from the Department of School Medical Services to the Ministry of Education, and also the close liaison required at state level between the National Fitness Organizers and education departments. However, following the example of Western Australia, the states took a different route, granting the State Councils for National Fitness the status of statutory bodies over the next decade and a half, and in the 1970s absorbing the functions of the Councils into state government departments of sport and recreation.[58]

If arguments for using mass physical exercising to militarist or eugenicist ends were expressed by a small but noisy minority of Australians in the late 1930s, after the Second World War these arguments were attributed to extremists and dangerous fanatics. Already, before the war, significant momentum had been gained by proponents of the view that sport and exercise could and should be liberating activities, wholesome and enjoyable ways to spend leisure time. After the war, the State Councils were well placed to develop this new view of physical activity with their emphasis on youth, sport and outdoor physical recreation. While the links to medicine, health and national fitness conferred on the Councils a legitimacy they may otherwise have lacked in these early days, their real connections lay within education. We should not be surprised, then, to find that a parallel shift in discourse on the body had been taking place in schools.

The New Physical Education

This shift in discourse on schooling bodies can be traced through a range of developments, none more obvious than the increasing tendency to substitute the term physical education for physical training. L.P. Jacks's books on the *Education of the Whole Man* (1931) and *Education through Recreation* (1932)[59] were widely read in Australia and Britain and provided timely arguments consistent with a new wave of child-centred progressivism in primary school education that the whole child must be educated and that the physical and emotional dimensions of development were just as important as the cognitive. In Victoria, the term physical education began to be used in the annual Ministry of Education reports from 1929 to express the emerging view of a 'subject' that included, as we noted in Chapter 5, 'not merely formal physical exercises, but swimming, organized games, rhythmic exercises, folk dancing, practical hygiene, and remedial exercises based on the medical assessment of the needs of each child'.[60]

A number of developments within the field supported this shift towards use of the term physical education and the broader notions it implied. We learned in Chapter 5 of the growing influence of the games ethic and sport in a new conception of physical education. In addition to this development, in Britain teachers trained in the private colleges for women had begun to experiment with rhythmic developments of Dano-Swedish gymnastics following the work of Carlquist and Falk in Scandinavia and Marsh in England, changes to established practices that were nevertheless gradual and hard won.[61] In Australia, the lack of a critical mass of trained gymnastics teachers allowed room for innovation untrammelled by the conservatism of the British scene, though as Wright[62] has noted, in Australia as in Britain a distinctively female approach to physical education was to be increasingly marginalized by the male discourses of science and sport during the post-Second World War period. However, between the wars, women such as Rosalie Virtue in Victoria and Ella Gormley in New South Wales worked hard to establish forms of physical training that involved less regimentation, especially for younger children and girls.

In 1933, on the subject of physical exercises for senior school girls, Virtue was emphatic that 'quick and informal methods of organization should be employed. Drill has no place in the daily physical training lesson for school girls.'[63] Eleven years earlier, she had issued guidelines to teachers of infants, and in these we can see the basis of future developments that gave equal weight to social and biological factors in physical education. She noted that 'anything in the way of formal gymnastics is, of course, out of place. But the play movements may be utilized and controlled in such a way as to keep, and considerably increase, their effect of happiness and enjoyment . . . . By the time the children leave the infants' school, they should also have had some definite training in a good standing position . . . be able to keep definite rhythm in such movements as marching, running, dancing steps, and jumps, and know something of what is meant by "fair play"'.[64]

Virtue was especially keen to utilize music to enhance the rhythmic qualities of movement, and she was a strong advocate of folk dancing as a key part of primary school physical education. Her ideas on folk dancing based on her work during the previous two decades were published in a series of articles in 1941. She argued that 'dancing, especially folk dancing, is now recognised as a most important form of the realisation and expression of music. The dancer must be able to study and appreciate a tune and use full mental and physical powers to express it in concerted motion.' She placed great emphasis on 'flowing' movements so that 'the dance should be regarded as a continuous whole with a character of its own, not as a succession of separate movements'.[65] She claimed that folk dancing put children in touch with their British heritage: 'English folk dancing has its roots in English folk lore. Children will be interested in much of its history and through it will acquire an atmosphere for their dancing. They will also become acquainted with one of the characteristic aspects of the social history of the English people.'[66] Such was the popularity of folk dancing in primary schools across Australia that the State Councils for National Fitness began from the early 1940s to collect and print folk dances for use by teachers, and there were regular folk dancing radio broadcasts to schools from the late 1940s.[67]

This sort of innovative work of Virtue in Victoria and female physical educators in the other states began to chip away at the orthodoxies of drilling and exercising during the 1920s and 1930s. The withdrawal in 1931 of the federally funded scheme of physical training linked to cadet training left the state governments with sole responsibility for the provision of physical education in their schools. In Victoria, the specialist staff servicing primary schools rose in numbers from two in 1935 to twenty-two in 1938, and the swimming branch grew from one to thirteen permanent instructors. In the state-controlled secondary schools, there were an additional twenty specialist physical education staff. Other states followed suit though at varying rates.[68]

126

However, school practice through the 1930s had yet to respond to this growth in staff numbers and the emergence of a new conception of physical education. Late in 1939 a Committee of the State Council for National Fitness in Victoria was appointed with authority to investigate the status and efficiency of physical education and to furnish recommendations concerning future practice.[69] Over 400 teachers from all types of schools responded to a survey of current practice. The survey produced a list of factors that the Committee felt impeded progress towards implementation of a new view of physical education, including a low regard for physical training among teachers, inadequate and unsatisfactory accommodation and equipment, insufficient medical supervision of students, the need for more specialist teachers, poor training of classroom teachers in the methods and practice of physical education, lack of awareness of the needs of adolescent girls, and parents' lack of knowledge of the importance of physical education.

The Committee summarized these responses in their Report and suggested there were different views of physical education among the teachers surveyed, including the use of physical activity as a means of developing a high degree of regimentation, as a medium for the correction of physical defects, for the development of a muscular physique and athletic prowess, and as gymnastic exercises with apparatus. The Committee's own view was very much at odds with these rival interpretations and in accord with the emerging notion of physical education as an essential part of general education, and the idea that the emphasis needed to shift from a biological perspective (education of the physical) to a social perspective (education through the physical).

The Report of this Victorian Committee on Physical Education attracted attention from other quarters. In September 1942, Bert Apps, the federal Organizer of National Fitness wrote to Mr Leach, Chief Inspector of Primary Schools in the Victorian Education Department, that the Report presented 'such a sane conception of the position that physical education should occupy in the general school curriculum, both from the point of view of emphasis and time, that it represents a valuable contribution to the physical education literature available in Australia'.[70] However, support such as this was not uniform, nor was this new conception of schooling bodies understood or accepted by everyone concerned. Official Victorian government reports for the period 1940 to 1946, which with few exceptions tended to portray developments in the most optimistic light possible, tell a story of incremental change, with much unevenness across the state in terms of the availability of and access to facilities, equipment and teaching expertise consistent with the new physical education. Across Australia, this process of slow and uneven change was magnified by the drain on resources caused by the war and the 'tyranny of distance'. Moreover, while instruction in games

and sports became a major component of timetabled physical activity lessons
after the Second World War, competitive sport continued to be organized
on a voluntary basis by non-specialists as an extra-curricular activity. And
as games and sport gradually began to take up increasing amounts of lesson
time, their presence in the curriculum for all children in government schools,
not just the minority of older children in high schools, required a rationale.

A step towards providing this rationale was taken by L.G. 'Huck'
Hamilton, assistant to Rosalie Virtue and later to become Organizer of
Physical Education with the Victorian Education Department, in a series of
articles that appeared in the 1941 edition of the Victorian *Education Gazette
and Teachers' Aid*. In one article titled 'Games Practice: its place and value
in the school', Hamilton addressed directly his concerns over the excesses
of the private school cult of athleticism and advocated instead the idea that
games were the means by which every child could be given an interest in
physical activity. He proposed that children should be taught to gain
satisfaction from seeing their own improvement in performance and not
necessarily from competing. He argued for a humanistic approach to sport-
based physical education where 'it must not be thought that the object of
games practice is to produce champions in sport. . . . There is a tendency in
many large schools to concentrate on the instruction of the few already
competent and gifted children, allowing this limited number to represent
the school in inter school competitive games. . . . One of the chief aims
[should be] to ensure that each and every child is given an opportunity to
learn games and to become to some degree skilled in them. In this way he
is assured of a healthy physical exercise with a definite motivating interest.'[71]

In Hamilton's comments we can note an important development in
thinking about schooling bodies through liberalized physical education. We
can detect the emergence of a form of the games ethic, discussed in some
detail in the previous chapter, and its reconstruction for use in the schooling
of the working classes. Once the preserve of social elites, games and sports
now had to be justified as a part of the education of all children in which the
children compete, not against each other but, in keeping with child-centred
doctrine, against themselves. In the education of the socially privileged,
games were a palpable sign of their social superiority. For the working
classes games playing was reconceptualized as a common denominator in
society that offered the same opportunities for healthful and enjoyable
physical activity to all.

This rationale for a new physical education built on humanistic, child-
centred principles that had games and sports at its core was expressed in
some detail five years later on the publication of a new syllabus for
Victorian schools, a text that was also widely used in other states. In his
letter to Mr Leach, Apps had noted that the Victorian Committee on
Physical Education had made no mention of a syllabus. He asked, 'is the

English 1933 Green Book the accepted one, and is it supplied to all schools?' and went on to express his view that 'it is the finest syllabus that has ever been produced and it has been made the basis of physical education in many other parts of the world'. By 1946, Apps's question was answered with the publication of a new textbook on physical education which was to be known as 'the Grey Book' in contrast to 'the Green Book'. One of the purposes of the Grey Book was to break away from British influences in physical education by presenting material that was appropriate for Australian and Victorian schools.

In the foreword to this new Victorian textbook,[72] the Chief Medical Inspector of Schools, H.P. Kelly, contrasted the new physical education with the drilling and exercising form of physical training the Grey Book sought to displace, arguing, as we saw at the beginning of this chapter, that 'formal exercises are artificial, unrelated to life situations, and generally lacking in interest'. Kelly went on to map out the key dimensions of this definition of physical education in which enjoyment and enthusiasm are recognized as beneficial outcomes of participation in physical activity, in contrast to the formality of the former regime of drilling and exercising. Accepting the notion that play is a 'natural activity' for children, Kelly commented that 'every child has the right to play, and this right must be restored to all children who have lost it'. In a significant conceptual leap, Kelly went on to equate 'play', within this new notion of physical education, with playing competitive team games.

> The only logical approach to this ideal is to adopt the method of providing physical education by teaching participation in games . . . . Physical values aside, the spirit of the game is invaluable as a means for developing social and moral character. The boy who learns to 'play the game' will be modest in victory and cheerful in defeat. Selfishness and cheating have no place in properly conducted games, while co-operation, courage, and self-confidence are developed.

In one stroke, Kelly had conflated the key elements of the games ethic of the privileged classes with the humanists' notion of the educational value of play, through the idea that all children in government schools had the right to participate in competitive team games. This was a significant conjoining of concepts underpinning the new approach to schooling bodies, since it positioned sport as pivotal to the educational legitimation of physical education. This conceptualization also had considerable symbolic power invoking as it does a natural and liberated body engaged in the enjoyable pastime of sport.

This new textbook and the liberalized notion of schooling bodies it promoted formed the basis of the work of growing numbers of specialist physical educators after the war. In 1944, six men and 24 women formed the staff of the Physical Education Branch in Victoria. By 1946, these numbers had swollen to 35 women and 25 men and by the end of the decade the staff comprised 30 women and 44 men.[73] This emerging body of specialist teachers of physical education very quickly saw their main role as developers of the skills pupils would use to participate in the team games offered by schools. Within this view of their role, physical education began to be positioned towards the end of the 1940s as the 'foundation stone' for children's participation in sport, as the site in which the skills required for sports participation should be developed.[74] With growing numbers of specialist advisers in the primary school sector and specialist physical education teachers in the secondary schools, it was now becoming possible to provide instruction for all children in the skills considered to be prerequisite to games playing. The specialists took on this role with considerable enthusiasm. In so doing, and despite the attempts of Hamilton and others to advocate against ultra-competitiveness, physical education began to be conceptualized as the base of a pyramidal structure which had elite sports competition at the top. The majority of children participated in school physical education, while only a very few talented individuals survived to reach the pinnacle of the pyramid. Physical education lessons provided the 'fundamental motor skills' of running, throwing, jumping, kicking and so on, and these were then applied within an ascending scale of competitive contexts in inter-school, inter-district, inter-state and international sport.

Liberated Bodies

One of the most significant influences on school practices of the campaigns for mass physical recreation in both Australia and Britain was that pupils' school experiences were of value if they could stimulate an interest in physical activity on into adulthood. The work of the State Councils for National Fitness in Australia and of organizations such as the Central Council for Physical Recreation in Britain created opportunities hitherto unknown for youth and young adults to participate in recreative physical activity, and teachers were exhorted to prepare children for an active adulthood. Rosalie Virtue suggested in 1946 that 'the impulse to play must be fostered in them so that many more than at present will later on frequent recreation playgrounds and will be familiar with enough activities to enable them to make the best use of the facilities provided there', while Huck Hamilton in a similar vein argued that 'one of the important contributions the school can make to the child's life is to give him an abiding interest in beneficial physical activities . . . the program to be satisfactory must include activities of the type in which children will want to engage during their out of school hours and more important still in their post school days'.[75]

The idea that young people leaving school may wish to continue their participation in the physical activities offered as part of the school curriculum required a major shift in the discourse in which these school practices were embedded. In addition to the actual changes in the activities themselves, particularly with the increasing opportunities to play games and to participate in activities such as camping, these activities could be presented as enjoyable and fun to do. The same could clearly not have been said for drilling and exercising, nor could the same relationship between school and society, school life and adult life, have been proposed.

It was stressed earlier in this chapter that the changes in public discourse emerging in the decade or so that straddled the Second World War had uneven effects both in the sphere of community action in relation to recreative physical activity and in school practice. But there is some evidence in these events nevertheless to suggest that a sea change of sorts was taking place, and that a looser form of power over the body had begun to insinuate itself in the process of schooling bodies. Despite the urgings of physical educators such as Virtue that there was no longer a place for the coercive disciplining of children through drill, despite the vision and the progressivism of the Grey Book, and the advances made through the work of the national fitness councils, drilling and exercising continued to be practised in schools in some Australian states until the 1960s. But these practices were increasingly viewed as anachronistic, belonging to people other than ourselves, with different purposes and ends in mind, as accidental remnants of another time. We may wish to question though the extent to which this new regime of the body and the looser form of power it entails might be viewed as a liberation of bodies. Is it not merely another form of corporeal power, in which the locus of regulation has shifted, but which is in many ways far harder to resist than the patently obvious attempts to coerce conformity of behaviour displayed by drilling and exercising? It is to consideration of this question that we turn in the next and concluding chapter.

Notes and References

1 Kelly, H.P. (1946) Medical Inspector of Schools, in Education Department of Victoria *Physical Education for Victorian Schools* Melbourne: Wilke.
2 Senator Foll, Minister for Health, in the *Sydney Sun*, 3 December 1938.
3 Gray, R. (1979) *The First Forty Years: The National Fitness and Community Recreation Councils of Western Australia 1939–1978* Department of Youth, Sport and Recreation, Western Australia.
4 *The Age*, 12 August 1938.

5 For example, see correspondence in A461/1 E347/1/11.
6 Ramsay, A. and Johnson, M. (1936) *Physical Education in Victoria* Melbourne: ACER.
7 Kentish, G. (1983) *Fritz Duras: The Father of Physical Education in Australia* Adelaide: ACHPER.
8 Kentish, *Fritz Duras*, pp. 46–7.
9 See A461/1 E347/1/11, letter dated 6 February 1939 from the ANZAAS, arguing for the urgent necessity of academic training in physical education; letter dated 23 February 1939 from the Association of Rhodes Scholars in relation to the need for properly trained physical educators.
10 Kirk, D. (1992) *Defining Physical Education: The Social Construction of a School Subject in Postwar Britain* London: Falmer.
11 A1928/1 783/3, letter dated 16 June 1937 from C.E.W. Bean to Dr Cumpston, Director-General of Health.
12 A1928/1 783/3 Section 1, letter dated 7 July 1938 from Professor G.S. Browne to Dr Cumpston, Director-General of Health.
13 *Parliamentary Debates*, 3 December 1936, p. 2833.
14 Billy Hughes in Walker, D. (1987) Mind and body, in Gammage, B. and Spearritt, P. (eds) *Australians 1938* Broadway: Fairfax, Syme and Weldon Associates, p. 227.
15 A461/1 E 347/1/11, 16 May 1938, comment from *The Age*.
16 A461/1 E 347/1/11, 13 December 1938.
17 A461/1 E 347/1/11, 16 May 1938, comment from *The Age*.
18 A1928 783/3 Section 1, 25 April 1938.
19 A1928 783/3 Section 1, 23 May 1938.
20 A1928 783/3 Section 1, 6 June 1938.
21 A1928 783/3 Section 1, 15 June 1938.
22 A1928 783/3 Section 1, 26 July 1938.
23 A1928 783/3 Section 1, 16 August 1938.
24 A1928 783/3 Section 1, 29 August 1938.
25 A1928 783/3 Section 1, 31 October 1938.
26 *Hansard*, 19 May 1938.
27 *Hansard*, 28 June 1938.
28 *Argus*, 13 October 1938, p. 1; Morris, E.S. (1939) Physical education in relation to national fitness, in *ANZAAS Report 24: Section 1 – Medical Science and National Health: Presidential Address*, pp. 194–8, 215–8.
29 *Argus*, 18 November 1938.
30 *The Age*, 17 November 1938.
31 *Argus*, 3 December 1938.
32 *Sydney Sun*, 3 December 1938.
33 *Argus*, letter from 'Faustus', 10 January 1939, p. 4.
34 *Argus*, letter from Angela Booth, 13 January 1939, p. 7.
35 Returned Services League correspondence in A461/1 E347/1/11, 29 November 1938; Australian Natives Association correspondence in A461/1 E347/1/11, 16 January 1939.
36 *Argus*, 7 March 1939, p. 2.
37 *Argus*, 14 December 1938, p. 8.
38 A1928/1 783/3, 19 November 1938.
39 A1928/1 783/5 Section 1, 8 March 1939.

40 Sutton, H, (1939) Physical education and national fitness *Australian Rhodes Review*, **4**, pp. 56–63.

41 Editorial on National fitness *Medical Journal of Australia*, 6 August 1938, p. 209.

42 Macintyre, S. (1986) *The Oxford History of Australia (Volume 4): The Succeeding Age, 1901–1942* Melbourne: Oxford University Press, pp. 330–2.

43 A461/1 E347/1/11, Part 3, Resolutions of the Commonwealth Coordinating Council for Physical Fitness, Inaugural Meeting, Melbourne, 5–6 January 1939.

44 A1928/1 783/5, 8 March 1939, Notice to Cabinet from Senator H.S. Foll, Minister for Health.

45 *Argus*, 7 January 1939, p. 7.

46 A461/1 E347/1/11, Part 3, Resolutions of the National Coordinating Council for Physical Fitness, Second Meeting, Canberra, 2 May 1939.

47 A461/1 E347/1/11, Part 1, Senator Foll to PM, 24 January 1939.

48 A461/1 E347/1/11, Part 1, 13 March 1939, Premier SA to PM.

49 Macintyre, *The Oxford History*, p. 330.

50 *The Age*, 10 April 1939; A461/1 E347/1/11, Part 1, 23 May 1939, Sir Frederick Stewart.

51 *The Age*, 5 June 1939, p. 9.

52 A461/1 E347/1/11, Part 3, Resolutions of the Commonwealth Council for National Fitness, Third Meeting, Melbourne, 27 July 1939.

53 A461/1 E347/1/11, Part 3, Minute for the Commonwealth Council for National Fitness, 25 May 1939.

54 A1928/1 783/5 Section 2, Physical Fitness General, 1941–1943.

55 *Parliamentary Debates*, 25 June 1941, p. 371.

56 E.g. A461/1 E347/1/11, Part 1, Report of the Commonwealth Council for National Fitness. Eighth Session Held in Melbourne on 25–26 October 1945.

57 A/461/1 E347/1/11, Part 1, Report of the Commonwealth Council, p. 5.

58 Deane, J.W. (1982) The development of the Department of Youth, Sport and Recreation in the State of Victoria. Unpublished MEd Thesis, University of Liverpool.

59 Jacks, L.P. (1931) *Education of the Whole Man* London: University of London Press; Jacks, L.P. (1932) *Education Through Recreation* London: University of London Press.

60 Minister of Public Instruction (1929) *Education Report for the Year 1928–9* Melbourne: Government Printer, p. 8.

61 Kirk, *Defining Physical Education*.

62 Wright, J. (1996) Mapping the discourses in physical education *Journal of Curriculum Studies*, **28** (3), pp. 331–51.

63 Education Department of Victoria *Education Gazette and Teachers' Aid*, May 1933.

64 Education Department of Victoria *Education Gazette and Teachers' Aid*, January 1922.

65 Education Department of Victoria *Education Gazette and Teachers' Aid*, November 1941.

66 Education Department of Victoria *Education Gazette and Teachers' Aid*, December 1941.

67 See reports of the Minister for Public Instruction during the late 1940s.

68 Crawford, R. (1981) A history of physical education in Victoria and New South Wales 1872–1939: with particular reference to English precedent. Unpublished PhD Thesis, La Trobe University.

69 Report of the Departmental Committee on Physical Education, Special Case File 892/P1, National Fitness Council 1941–1956, Series 892, Unit 81, No. 13, National Fitness Council of Victoria.

70 Apps's letter to Leach, in Special Case File 892/P1, National Fitness Council 1941–1956, Series 892, Unit 81, No. 13, National Fitness Council of Victoria.

71 Hamilton, L.G. (1941) Games practice: Its place and value in the school *Education Gazette and Teachers' Aid*, July 1941.

72 Education Department of Victoria *Physical Education for Victorian Schools*.

73 Minister of Public Instruction (1945) *Education Report for the Year 1944–45* Melbourne: Government Printer, p. 24; Minister of Public Instruction (1947) *Education Report for the Year 1946–47* Melbourne: Government Printer, p. 7; Minister of Public Instruction (1950) *Education Report for the Year 1949–50* Melbourne: Government Printer, p. 21.

74 Cf. Evans, J. (1990) *Sport in Schools* Geelong: Deakin University Press.

75 Virtue, R. (1946) The physical education of school children *Education Magazine*, September, p. 150; Hamilton, Games practice.

Conclusion

I have argued along with Philip Corrigan that 'bodies matter schooling'. Indeed, the regulation of children's bodies has been of such major significance, I have suggested, that it may be viewed legitimately as a defining characteristic of schooling since the inauguration of compulsory mass elementary education. Many forms of school practice contribute to the process of schooling bodies, but there are some practices that have a more specific relationship to this process than others. This study has explored the emergence and interrelationships between the 1880s and the 1940s of three of these practices, physical training, medical inspection and school sport and games.

I have argued that changes to these specialized school practices provide insights into shifts in public discourse and shifts in forms of biopower during this period. Drilling and inspecting children's bodies with precision and obsessive attention to detail seemed appropriate within public discourse concerned with the problems of social order and economic productivity, public health and racial deterioration, Anglo-Celtic national identity and Australia's relationship with Britain. Drilling and inspecting children's bodies may have appeared to be 'heavy, ponderous, meticulous' expressions of power, as coercive and unpleasant ways of regulating behaviour. It is true that they were explicitly motivated by power brokers' and policy-makers' concerns to ensure that there was a sound return for the investment of public money in schooling in the form of healthy, compliant yet productive citizens. But these practices were also optimistic expressions of the idea that schools were key sites for educational and medical interventions that could prevent much human misery before it had a chance to manifest itself. Whatever else this project involved, schooling bodies through drilling and examining them at least took a positive and hopeful view of Australia's future and counted the climate and environment to be an asset that Britain, the 'mother country', lacked.

By the end of the First World War, this optimism seems already to have vanished as public discourse shifted to accommodate attempts to make sense of the turmoil that beset Australian society during the war and the peace that followed. Not only did the war expose the social class and religious divides within Australian society, which were as we saw vividly portrayed by conflict surrounding sport, but it also contributed to a climate of bluntly repressive, authoritarian and conservative politics, industrial strife and economic depression. It seems almost as if the optimism of the pre-war era was no longer thought to be worth the effort, even though some, such as the school medical officers in Victoria, remained true to their pre-war convictions. The net result of this profound shift in public discourse for the practices that sought to school bodies through drilling and examining them was that they produced resisting rather than docile bodies, bodies that were disinclined to be subjected to coercive regimes of regulation.

Yet through this postwar turmoil, the notion that playing games and sports was a means of both civilizing and liberating the bodies of all children began gradually to impress itself on educational policy-makers. This apparent enthusiasm of education bureaucrats, politicians and teachers for games playing in educational settings is in some ways puzzling, since many had their own firsthand experiences of the ugly excesses of the cult of athleticism to draw on. It would have been patently obvious to them that playing games did not necessarily have a civilizing effect on the young men and women who had had the benefits of schooling in elite educational institutions, and it was not uncommon for some to speak out against these excesses. But even those educationists and others who had seen and understood the dark underside of sport competition nevertheless remained steadfast in their views that participation in games could have a beneficial civilizing effect on working-class children. Since these games and sports were so unlike the 'heavy, ponderous, meticulous' drilling and exercising that was the staple form of physical activity for the majority of working-class children, it may not be too difficult to see why they might also have been viewed as liberating experiences for these children.

Of course, for many children, participation in sport, particularly in competitive team games, was no less a hazardous and harrowing experience than drilling and exercising. But as many historians of sport, chief among them J.A. Mangan, have now shown convincingly, the games ethic was a powerful educational ideology that was able to transcend otherwise obdurate and impermeable boundaries of class, race and national identity. For some, the advocates, this robustness was merely confirmation of their belief that games and sports are a form of common currency among all civilized people, no better example being Baron De Coubertin's deep admiration for the sporting pursuits of the English public schools that shaped his re-invention of the Olympic Games. For others, the sceptics, the excesses of games and sports confirmed their deep-seated disdain for the merely physical side of human nature and their firm belief that is was dangerous to let the animal passions of young men and women run wild.

Between these extreme positions we can perhaps steer a course that provides a more satisfactory explanation as to why games and sports were promoted with such enthusiasm by educators and why they came to form the basis not only of school physical education for the masses after the Second World War in Australia and in Britain, but also of the national fitness campaigns that nearly managed to encompass a broader, health-focused agenda only to be reduced to mass physical recreation movements that were almost solely concerned with physical activities in educational settings.

According to Crawford, the public schools of Australia retained some elements of the British version of the games ethic, but during the first three decades of the twentieth century added their own virtues to provide a distinctively Australian flavour.

> If the Australian public schools had sought in the 19th century to imitate a major strand of English educational life and mirror the ideals of middle and upper class sport, they were in the 20th century to assert a value system which was inimitably of strong native invention. Teamwork, comradeship, leadership and courage would remain as indelible qualities to be drawn from playing games but the distinctive Australian ethos of self-reliance and manliness came to have equal importance. The image of the tough, independent, strong and passionate winner in sporting contests endeared to the wide cross section of the sporting community found its own niche in the Public School and produced its own stereotypes.[1]

While this reconstruction of the games ethic in the Australian public schools may indeed have reflected some indigenous qualities of Australian manhood, these same virtues did not necessarily apply to the working classes. Games as a form of leadership education was not a key concern in the education of the working classes in the way that it was for the middle classes and, in particular, for boys who would go on to take up positions of responsibility in government, business, the professions and the armed services. Nevertheless, notions of manliness which contained the key features of appropriately heterosexual masculine behaviour were prominent in early justifications of games for boys in government schools.

Following the First World War there was an emphasis on physical development through games and other physical activities in an attempt to repair 'the national physique'.[2] Later, through the 1920s, we find greater attention being paid to values such as cooperation, courage, and playing for the sake of the team, as much as means of counteracting undesirable behaviour, like cheating, than as positive virtues in themselves. Later still, in the 1930s and 1940s, under the influence of the progressive movement in primary school education and perhaps in more conscious consideration of girls in addition to boys, concepts such as self-confidence, enjoyment and play begin to be added to the list of positive qualities games were claimed to foster.

Mention was made in Chapter 5 that some groups had a substantial stake in the successful growth of team games in government schools. The Victorian Football League, for instance, lent considerable support to inter-school sport. However, their interest was not entirely altruistic. As an organization of professional sportsmen the VFL, and its professional counterparts in other states and other football codes, regarded the state schools as prime breeding grounds for stars of the future. The final crystallization of the notion that government schools could provide the raw materials for elite sport appeared in the 1940s as increasing numbers of specialist instructors in physical education began to be employed by the physical education branches of various state Education Departments and physical education lessons came to be seen as the place to teach basic sports skills.

It has also been noted that the government high schools, in a manner similar to the English Grammar Schools of the Edwardian era described by Mangan, were able to use the games ethic and games playing to some effect in a process of social emulation and distancing. This use of games was of less relevance to the government primary schools of the interwar period, since they were not in direct competition with the private schools in the same way as were the high schools. Nevertheless, before the expansion of mass secondary education in the post-Second World War period, the state high schools were the flagships of the government school systems, and their influence on the primary sector cannot be dismissed. Particularly in the country areas where we have noted in Chapter 5, through McKernan's work, that the values inherent in the games ethic received considerable support, the high schools' approach to sport had a significant impact on primary schools. For the urban working classes, this influence may have been less noticeable since the high schools serviced the lower strata of the middle classes.

It is open to question whether the use of the games ethic to justify working-class children's right to participate in games was an expression of profound egalitarian sensibilities. As part of the popular mythology of Australian national identity,[3] egalitarianism may have been a factor in the use of the games ethic to justify sport in government schools. Daly has suggested that 'Australian sport has always catered for the masses. Community sport is available to anybody and everybody. Few sports are class orientated and the climate and natural facilities encourage most to participate from an early age.'[4] The evidence presented in Chapters 5 and 6, particularly in relation to lack of available facilities for the urban working classes during the interwar period and beyond, calls into question this view.

In the context of such a powerful mythology,[5] there is no actual requirement for egalitarian sentiment to be widespread in Australian society, but, more importantly, it was widely believed that Australians should, by and large, have 'a fair go'.[6] The strategic use of rhetoric by games enthusiasts that appealed to such sentiments would have made sense if egalitarianism was likely to resonate with the sentiments of government and educational policy-makers. In some cases, it may indeed have done so. However, in the socially conservative climate of the 1920s and 1930s in Australia, where the extension of charity to other less privileged social groups became less likely,[7] this factor cannot completely account for government and bureaucratic support for games playing during the interwar period, though it may explain why ordinary Australians, teachers among them, considered that 'every child had a right to play'.

While the various shifts in the ways in which the games ethic was applied to sport in government schools can be noted, it is also clear that the development of social and moral character of working-class children was a matter of enduring concern throughout this period. Concerns over racial degeneration and the survival of a white race in the southern hemisphere were taken seriously by many educated Australians during the 30 years leading up to the First World War, as they were in the United States and Britain, and these concerns fed ongoing debates over Australian nationhood. The social tensions that surfaced during the war identified by Michael McKernan's work show that the fears of the educated classes over the lack of a stable national identity were not entirely groundless. As we saw in Chapter 4, the project of social regulation through medical and other interventions fell out of favour after the war. However, it is not inconceivable that politicians, government bureaucrats and other social leaders, themselves educated in the elite private schools and their imitators, considered that some form of control over the recreations of the urban working classes might bear fruit in terms of reducing the likelihood of class conflict.

Given the considerable class division centring on sport indicated by McKernan's work, and in particular the working-class use of games as a form of release from onerous responsibilities and duties, we might pause to wonder at the relevance of some of the high-sounding ideals surrounding games for the majority of children to whom they were intended to apply. The consistently bold statements of the games ethic in official government papers through the 1920s and 1930s need to be set beside the regular references in these statements to the need to counteract negative dimensions of sports participation. These references provide some indication that attempts to civilize the working classes through the benign influence of playing games the middle-class way were, at least, incomplete. The continuation of public and private concerns over inappropriate behaviour connected with sport in the elite public schools cannot have helped the case in relation to games in the government schools.[8] Nevertheless, the endurance of the games ethic over considerable spans of time and distance, and its durability within a range of different social and cultural conditions, is indicative of the immense power and appeal of the notion that participation in team games has, in ideal circumstances, a benign influence that can school bodies imbued with the values of civilized Australians.

There is another part to this explanation that lies, I suggest, in the forms of embodied public social interaction games and sports permitted that were in most other spheres of everyday life repressed or at least denied expression, particularly between males. Apart from the monotony, tedium and regimentation of drilling and exercising, gymnastics-based forms of physical training never really became mass recreational pastimes because they were intentionally designed to restrict and delegitimize any public social interaction that involved bodily contact. In Foucault's words, these systems of movement sought to minimize 'dangerous coagulations', perhaps as much for reasons of health and hygiene, or racial integrity, as for compliance with emotional and sexual mores. The obsessive concern to discipline the movement of bodies in space and time that is so clearly evident in these systems of drilling and exercising revealed public discourses that were overwhelmingly concerned with problems of social order in all its forms and produced solutions in systems of segregation and differentiation. The precise, detailed and meticulous drilling and examination of children's bodies seemed to present such solutions.

The notable exception to the tendency of Australians to resist such regimes of the body was, of course, the immense popularity of various forms of 'keep fit' among women. Keep-fit activities emerged during the 1920s and 1930s and drew extensively on modifications of Dano-Swedish gymnastics, usually set to music.[9] In considering the apparent contrast between this example and the growing enthusiasm for games and sports among men, we can perhaps speculate that this was a means of compensating for the severe restrictions on legitimate bodily contact between men that might take place publicly in a fiercely heterosexual society. Women, on the other hand, may have had less need for the forms of physical contact that games playing permitted since avenues for various legitimate bodily interactions in public were considered permissible.

As we saw in Chapter 5, the idea that games playing offered an antidote to homosexual activity among pupils in England's public schools was already widespread in elite school circles by the 1880s.[10] Games offered a cathartic release of emotional energy that could only with grave consequences, so it was held, be bottled up in adolescent males. Games seemed to offer some solutions to this problem of the illicit intermingling of male bodies, not by methods of segregation and differentiation, of keeping bodies apart, but by bringing them together in particular, socially sanctioned ways. Competitive team games are above all else public performances, often played in wide open, flat spaces where little or nothing of the performance can be hidden from the gaze of other players or spectators. Male bodies are permitted to make physical contact, but typically this contact is violent, the brutishness merely constrained but not disguised by formally agreed sets of rules. At the turn of the century, shaking hands in a 'manly' fashion, perhaps a firm pat on the back, were also permissible forms of bodily contact, means of offering congratulations or celebrating a goal or some other excellence in performance. It is not difficult to see how, in the heat of the contest, this rough physical contact between males, in states of high alertness and excitement, might offer an acceptable form of behaviour for male relating to male in public. In contrast to the strategy of segregating and outlawing any form of physical contact between males offered by drilling and exercising, games at least gave boys and men one avenue for socially approved bodily contact.

There was no need for this view of games, as a means of civilizing bodies and thereby ensuring the dominance of heterosexuality among males, to be articulated in this fashion for it to be influential. Indeed, it is only in the form of an unarticulated feeling for what is right that such a view could be influential at all. As a form of hegemonic ideology, the power of this view to shape the belief of so many educationists and politicians in the civilizing effects of games is in its unspokenness. The Minister of Education in England and Wales, Mr Lloyd, commenting on a 1956 Unesco report on 'The Place of Sport in Education', was expressing this distaste for analysing sport when he said that 'the English idea of sport is such that the English do not like professional, professorial discourses on sport'.[11] Too much scrutiny of games and sports might disturb the comfortable feeling that sport is an unambiguous social good, far removed from controversial social and political issues.

Regardless of whether or not the reader finds this explanation to be satisfactory or persuasive, there can be no argument about the role games and sports have played both in shaping school physical education and community physical recreation policies since the end of the Second World War. Countless surveys of school practices in Australia and Britain through the 1960s to 1980s have shown that competitive team games dominated physical education programmes and that sport in schools often dictated both the content of physical education lessons and the timing, in terms of when activities were offered, in keeping with seasonal variations in sports. Surveys of community participation in physical activities, in contrast, showed that relatively few adults continued to participate in major team games when they left school, and instead indulged themselves in the simpler pleasures of walking, swimming and fishing. Nevertheless, apart for the establishment of outdoor camps by the State Councils for National Fitness, much of the post-Second World War policy and planning in the area of community recreation focused on the provision of sports facilities and the promotion of participation in games and sports. It was only in the early 1970s and in recognition of the emerging concept of 'leisure' that the State Councils for National Fitness began to realize these policies may require revision. But for at least twenty years after the war, the priority for recreation planners was to provide facilities and encouragement for playing games and sports.[12]

While accepting that games have played a dominant role in school and community practices since the 1940s, we may still wish to argue over the extent to which this emerging force in physical culture might be viewed as a means of liberating bodies or whether it might simply be a new form of biopower. Certainly, against drilling and exercising, team games appear to offer quite contrasting experiences of physical activity; there are no words of command, no ranks or files and, most significant of all, in the most popular team sports such as football, cricket and so on, no need for precise attention to detail in the execution of a movement. Indeed, players are encouraged to be innovative, to employ novel combinations of movements in order to beat an opponent, and as we have already noted, particular forms of physical contact are sanctioned. These features of games may indeed suggest a 'looser form of power' over the body.

But this does not suggest that power has ceased to operate on and through bodies. As many games theorists have noted, games are rule-bound activities; it is the rules that provide games with their characteristic forms. These rules define the objective of the game, the kinds of movements players might perform, and the ways in which they can conduct themselves in relation to other players. Within the context of these rules, players and coaches devise techniques and strategies that may assist them to win the game. In most games, space is organized explicitly, from the drawing of boundary lines that contain the playing area to markings within the playing area that permit or prohibit actions or players entering or occupying the defined space. Time is also organized explicitly, from the drawing of a temporal boundary that defines when play is to begin and end to the timing of particular actions. Players who learn to play a game well submit themselves to this regulation of their bodies in time and space. The repetitive work that is required to achieve some degree of mastery of the techniques of games creates movement patterns that, once learned, tend to stay with the player, and may even influence and at times interfere with other movements, such as the squash player's difficulties with a tennis shot. It is even possible, indeed not uncommon, for highly practised techniques and strategies of movement to become dominant characteristics of a person's movements outside of the game.

Biopower is clearly operating within these matrices of regulated space and time that constitute games. Power has not disappeared in this new form of physical activity that replaced drilling and exercising, but it has changed along with the form of the activity. In traditional competitive team games and many more recently developed and popular sports, a level of individualization of movement is tolerated and in some cases encouraged. Individualism would never have been possible in drilling and exercising, where the synchronized execution of movements *en masse* was at the heart of the process of schooling bodies.

It is also the case that the new form of biopower involved a shift in the locus of regulation, from a predominantly though not exclusively external source to a predominantly though not exclusively internal source. Drilling and exercising depended heavily on the instructor issuing the words of command, and on prompt obedience to these commands on the part of the child. Calisthenic exercising required little critical interpretation on the part of the child of the instructor's commands or of the environment in which the exercises had to be performed: obedience was everything. The games player, in contrast, needs to be able to make sense of patterns of play and to select field or court positions and movements appropriate to the phase of the game and the multiple configurations of other players. While an instructor-centred approach remains common in contemporary school physical education, good games players need to take a level of responsibility for their own learning that was entirely absent in drilling and exercising. In this respect, the locus of corporeal regulation has shifted away from the teacher as an external and coercive source of power over the body to the learner who, if she is participating wholeheartedly and seriously in playing the game, submits to the regime and regulates her own behaviour on its terms.

In addition to the individualization and internalization of biopower attendant on the rise to prominence of games and sports in school and community settings, the massification of physical recreation has led to the greater diffusion of this looser form of power over the body. As increasing numbers of people experienced sport-based school physical education, and as awareness of opportunities for and the desirability of physical recreational activity became more widespread, so the newer form of biopower is diffused throughout society. People need not be actively involved in physical recreation to feel the effects of biopower. Even those who lead sedentary lives may have found it hard to remain unaware of and unaffected by the many campaigns advocating the desirability of an active lifestyle and may have been unable to avoid feelings of guilt and anxiety over their sedentariness.

Many other factors may now, in the 1990s, be implicated in accentuating the individualization, internalization and diffusion of biopower as public discourse is constituted by debates over globalization and technologization, environmentalism and flexible capital accumulation, healthism and visualcy. The increasing prominence of idealized bodies in the visual media and through advertising may be prominent among these factors, as may new dietary regimes and medical practices. Notwithstanding the importance of these recent developments and the need for their careful analysis, I suggest that in Australia perhaps even more so than in Britain, the emergence of games in the postwar era as a new form of schooling bodies signalled the imminent arrival of a profound shift in biopower. While competitive team games had formed a central plank in the educational ideologies of socially elite schools for both boys and girls in Australia and Britain since the late nineteenth century, it was their incorporation into mass-school and community practices after the Second World War, and the reconstructions of the games ethic to accommodate this change, that heralded a major shift in the form of biopower.

Against the formality of drilling and exercising, games may have seemed to offer a liberating experience for the children able to make the direct comparison, or at the very least a freeing up of the processes of schooling bodies. Evidence from a wide and diverse range of sources would suggest that, against this notion, games have been unpleasant experiences for many children, particularly girls and women, that they would go to some lengths to avoid. The fact that the vast majority of adults never voluntarily played any form of team game or sport when they had left school would seem to add some weight to this observation. Yet these uncomfortable truths were scarcely if ever acknowledged in the policies and practices of school and community physical educators and educational policy-makers who would, I suspect, have been quite shocked and dismayed to learn, if they were capable of facing this truth, that playing games and sports was a deeply unpopular recreation for many people. Of course, they did accept, as many others with a mission in life do, that there are some who have yet to see the light. But their firm conviction was that once given the opportunity to participate in sport, the masses would be won over to the joys and delights of chasing a football around a field or swatting a ball with a racket. Instead, most of the Australian population who did develop an interest in sport preferred to be entertained by watching others performing rather than by playing themselves.

There are a number of features of games that make them potentially hazardous activities, from a participant's point of view. Key among these is that games can be violent, even when this physical aggression is contained within the rules, and injury is always a possibility. Games involve competing, a requirement that can be extremely stressful for some children. And perhaps even more important still is that games can be a humiliating experience since they demand a public demonstration of physical competence (or incompetence) that in turn exposes one's body to the critical scrutiny of others. In fact, it is these features of games playing, the very features that most recommended it to educationists in the first place, that render this activity a potentially hazardous one for so many participants. Some physical educators have recognized this, and have attempted through various means to humanize games. Moreover, feminist and pro-feminist physical educators have recognized the overtly masculinist nature of games and their origins as a strategy to confirm heterosexuality among boys and men. The extent to which these women and men can transform games in ways that make them more attractive to more children and adults and to provide a means of challenging rather than reinforcing compulsory heterosexuality remains to be seen.[13]

In the meantime, millions of young people have experienced forms of physical activity in schools, drilling and exercising and more recently, games and sports, that may have alienated them from rather than educated them in and about their bodies. For those resisting bodies, their physical education may have been experienced in the negative, as other to that formally sanctioned by society. Even for those who have found some corporeal liberation in games and sports, this regime of the body may be a source of chronic injuries and eventual disabilities, antisocial behaviour and neuroses.

One way in which these forms of schooling bodies may have been improved in the past and may still be improved in the future[14] is for social and educational theorists to begin to take serious note of the social construction of the body through schooling, and in particular through processes of physical education and sport. By bringing these school practices under detailed examination, by seeking out the connections between these practices and other related practices, by taking seriously the effects of these practices on young people, and by providing means of educating teachers, policy-makers and the general public about the whole range of consequences of school practices, perhaps the processes of schooling bodies may be less likely to be oppressive, negative, and alienating and more likely to be fulfilling, enabling and in the most hopeful sense of the word, liberating.

Notes and References

1 Crawford, R. (1981) A history of physical education in Victoria and New South Wales 1872–1939: with particular reference to English precedent. Unpublished PhD Thesis, La Trobe University, p. 400.

2 Crawford, R. (1981) A history of physical education, p. 378.

3 On the subject of Australian egalitarianism, see White, R. (1981) *Inventing Australia: Images and Identity 1688–1980* Sydney: George Allen & Unwin; Ward, R. (1966) *The Australian Legend* Melbourne: Oxford University Press, 2nd edn.

4 Daly, J.A. (1985) Structure, in *Australian Sport: A Profile* Canberra: Australian Government Printing Service, p. 15.

5 Barthes, R. (1972) *Mythologies* New York: The Noonday Press.

6 A common articulation of the link between Australian egalitarianism and sport appeared in the column of sports writer Jeff Wells: 'Play the game hard but fair. Help your mate. Work for your team. Don't bung on side. Give the other mob a

fair go too. No low mongrel acts. And have a couple together after the game', in Wells, *The Australian Weekend*, 28–9 April 1990.

7   Bacchi notes increasing resistance among the middle classes following the First World War to providing any form of economic support to the 'wastrels' they believed constitued the growing population of poor and unemployed, in Bacchi, C.L. (1980) The nature–nurture debate in Australia, 1900–1914 *Historical Studies*, **19**, pp. 199–212.

8   The behaviour of schoolboy spectators continued to attract public criticism into the 1930s when the heads of the six schools of the APS in Victoria were forced to ban 'frog dancing' and 'crocodile marching' at sports meetings, *Argus*, 21 June 1938. Further misbehaviour prompted calls to consider scaling down competitive sport due to the antics of supporters and the time lost to academic work for those boys involved in preparation for competition, *Argus*, 10 July 1939.

9   Cf. Matthews, J.J. (1987) Building the body beautiful *Australian Feminist Studies*, **5**, Summer, pp. 17–34.

10 Macintosh, P.C. (1968) *Physical Education in England Since 1800* London: Bell, (2nd edn); Mangan, J.A. (1981) *Athleticism in the Victorian and Edwardian Public School* Cambridge: Cambridge University Press.

11 In McIntosh, *Physical Education in England*, p. 281.

12 Cf. Deane, J.W. (1982) The Development of the Department of Youth, Sport and Recreation in the State of Victoria. Unpublished MEd Thesis, University of Liverpool.

13 For overviews of alternatives to traditional approaches to physical education, see Hellison, D. (1988) Our constructed reality: some contributions of an alternative perspective to physical education pedagogy *Quest*, **40** (1), pp. 84–90; Rovegno, I. and Kirk, D. (1995) Articulations and silences in socially critical work on physical education: toward a broader agenda *Quest*, **47** (4), pp. 447–74.

14 The consequences for contemporary and future programmes of school physical education of the arguments developed in this book have begun to be explored in Kirk, D. (1997) Schooling bodies for new times: the reform of school physical education in high modernity, in Fernandez-Balboa, J-M. (ed.) *Critical Aspects in Human Movement: Rethinking the Profession in the Postmodern Era* Albany, NY: SUNY Press.

Index

Index

Garton, S.   20–1
games ethic   91–6, 101, 105–7, 125, 128–9, 136–9
gender   1, 7, 70, 90
Greig, J.   58–60, 76, 80–2
Grey Book   129, 131
gymnastics   7–8, 12, 32, 34–6, 113, 140
    Ling System   33, 35, 42–3, 45, 53
    Swedish System   40, 45–6, 74, 97, 125, 140

Haller, M.   20
Hamilton, D.   12–13
Hamilton, L.G. 'Huck'   128, 130
heterosexuality   96–7, 140, 141, 145
heterosexual masculinity   98, 137
homosexuality   96, 140
Hoskins, K.   12–13
Hughes, W.M.   19, 37–8, 41, 115
humanistic approach   128

Immigration Restriction Act (1902)   115
    see also White Australia policy

Jacks, L.P.   125
junior cadet training   30, 37–8, 56, 70, 94, 99
Junior Cadet Training Manual (1916)   43–5, 53
Junior Cadet Training Scheme (1911–31)   55, 64, 67–8, 72–4, 76, 119

Ling, P.H.   8, 32
    see also gymnastics, Ling System
Lowenthal, D.   9

McKernan, M.   98–101, 138–9
McIntosh, P.C.   32, 40
maleness   7
Mangan, J.A.   91–2, 104, 136, 138
manliness   91, 94
masculinity   96
Mauss, M.   10–11
Medical Journal of Australia   77–80, 82, 120
Melbourne Conferences on Physical Training   39–43, 73
middle class
    Australians   100
    conceptions of competitive team games   107
    women   97
middle classes   99, 101, 138
militarism   8, 31, 67

Model Course of Physical Training (1902)   36, 40
modernity   3, 24–5, 90
Muskett, P.   22

nationhood   16, 18–19, 56, 107, 139
National Fitness Act (1941)   108, 112, 115, 124
National Health and Medical Research Council   115–17, 123
national identity   17, 68, 135–6, 138
nationalism   18, 67

postmodernity   10
power–knowledge   13
privileged classes   14, 89–90, 129
    see also bourgeoisie; middle classes; social elites

Royal Commission on Physical Training (Scotland)
    23, 30, 40, 42, 52–4

Searle, G.   73
Second World War   14–15, 25, 74, 89, 91, 107, 124–5, 128, 131, 137–8, 141, 144
Sherington, G.   93
social elites   91, 128
    see also privileged classes
Smith, W.D.   31
State Councils for National Fitness   121–5, 130, 141
Sutton, H.   41, 42, 43, 56–64, 69, 76, 120

Tate, F.   31, 40, 68–71, 77, 101, 103
Techow, G.   7–8, 32–3, 35–6,
Thomson, I.   32, 36
Turner, B.   13, 64

Victorian State Schools Amateur Athletics Association   34, 102–3, 105
Virtue, R.   74, 125–6, 128, 130–1

Weber, C.   40
White Australia policy   18, 37, 57
    see also Immigration Restriction Act
working class
    children   14, 136, 139
    pupils   101
    view of competitive sport   107
working classes   89, 99–100, 104, 128, 138

148